שייך ל ______________________

מס' סידורי __________

שם התלמיד	שנה	נמסר	הוחזר

THE SINGER EDITION

ספר
עשרת הדברות

ללמוד • לשמור • לעשות

Mitzvoth 25-38

The Fourteen Mitzvoth of the Asereth HaDibroth

THE RENNERT TARYAG MITZVAH PROJECT

Reproduction Requests, Taryag Legacy F oundation, Inc., 1136 Somerset Avenue, Lakewood, NJ 08701
phone. 732-942-3420, fax. 732-942-3630, email. curriculum@taryag.org

To contact a curriculum support associate please call: 1-888-4TARYAG (1-888-482-7924)

ISBN 1-933296-50-X

The Rennert Taryag Mitzvah Project

The Jewish people can achieve eternity only by perpetuating their Jewish heritage

We proudly dedicate
the Taryag Mitzvah Project,
a historic Torah educational initiative, to
The Children of Our Nation,
the future of the Jewish people

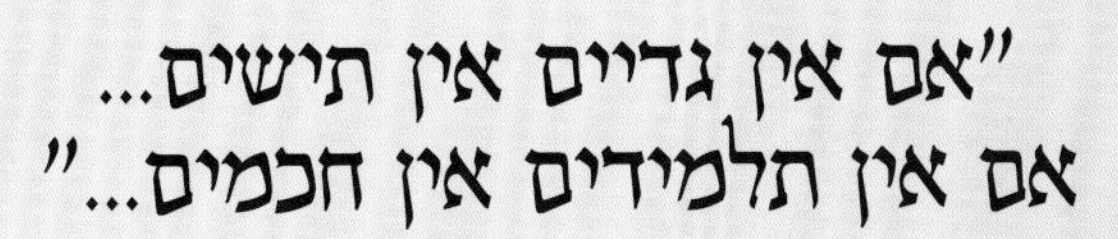

"אם אין גדיים אין תישים...
אם אין תלמידים אין חכמים..."

בראשית רבה, פרשה מב' אות ג'

*"Without kids, there are no goats…
Without students, there can be no scholars"*

*The Taryag Mitzvoth are the spiritual infrastructure
and framework for our lives.
Studying the Mitzvoth will inspire future generations
to be committed to our timeless heritage.
As the Taryag Mitzvoth are the heritage of all Jewish children,
we pray that this program will reach, teach, and enrich
every Jewish child in the world, regardless of community or background.*

Ira Leon & Ingeborg Rennert
Randy & Tamara Winn
Mitchell & Yonina Davidson
Ari & Erynne Rennert

This volume is lovingly dedicated to the memory of

RABBI YITZCHOK AHRON SINGER זצ"ל

by his wife

Rebbetzin Bluma Singer שתחי'

and children

Baruch and Susie Singer
Yitzchok Ahron

Eli Hersh and Rivki Singer
Naftali and Shevy Silber,
Yaakov Yisroel, Sholom Eliezer,
Moshe Aryeh Leib, Chaya Miriam,
Dovid Yecheskel, Devorah Leah

Nussie and Ruchy Singer
Avi and Yisroel

Yossie and Suri Singer
Mordechai, Naftali Meir,
Malka Charna

Yisroel Singer
Leah

לזכרון עולם

Rabbi Yitzchak Ahron Singer זצ״ל

A PASSION FOR TRADITION AND EXCELLENCE

With his imposing presence, meticulous attire, and eyes ablaze with wisdom, Rabbi Yitzchak Ahron Singer זצ״ל was the very image of the aristocratic rabbi of old. He was a towering Torah scholar, a scintillating and inspiring public speaker, and a man of nobility and refinement.

Descended from a long line of illustrious rabbis, Rabbi Singer was nonetheless, in a very real sense, a self-made man. His father, Rabbi Eliyahu Singer זצ״ל, was recognized as a tremendous *talmid chacham*. Rav Eliyahu was a *talmid muvhak* of Rabbi Sholom Mordechai Schwadron, the Berzhaner Rav, known to Jewish history as the great Maharsham. Rav Eliyahu was also very close with the Bluzhever Rebbe. When he passed away at the young age of forty-nine, he left writings on the entire Talmud, Bavli and Yerushalmi.

As a young boy growing up, Rabbi Singer was deeply influenced by his great father, but when his father passed away, he was left to develop further on his own, which he accomplished brilliantly. At a young age he became the Rabbi of the Belmont Avenue Synagogue in Newark, New Jersey. Subsequently, he was the Rabbi of a large shul called the Garden City Synagogue in Hartford, Connecticut, and later served for over forty years as the Rabbi of the Bialystok Shul on the Lower East Side.

Rabbi Singer was an excellent rabbi, a kind and gentle leader. He cared about everyone in his community and always made it his business to be there for them on their happy and not so happy occasions. He was also a masterful teacher. Over the years, he said in-depth *shiurim* on most of the Talmud and Poskim. He also said *shiurim* on Ein Yaakov on the Aggadic sections of the Talmud. His delivery was mesmerizing, and all his *shiurim* were well-attended. He was particularly famous as a passionate and eloquent speaker, especially in the Yiddish language, in which he had no peer. Always in high demand, he tried to accommodate everyone, even if it was at his own inconvenience.

Creating a bridge between the younger generations and the hallowed heritage of previous generations was one of the touchstones of Rabbi Singer's life. He always maintained warm and close associations with the leading rabbis of the generation, such as Rav Moshe Feinstein זצ״ל, the Bluzhever Rebbe זצ״ל, the Bobover Rebbe זצ״ל, the Satmar Rav זצ״ל and the Kapitchenitzer Rav זצ״ל. And he always made it a point to take his children to meet *gedolei Yisrael,* because he knew it was essential for their *chinuch.*

It is therefore entirely fitting that his name be associated in perpetuity with one of the most important advances in Torah and Jewish education in our times.

נר מצוה ותורה אור

Credits

Student Textbook

Editor-in-Chief
Rabbi Dovid Wax

General Editor
Mrs. Ahuva Weiss

Curriculum Review
Rabbi Nechemiah Gottlieb

Contributing Editors
Rabbi Shimon Finkelman
Rabbi Yitzchak Mandelkorn
Rabbi Moishe Bak

Editorial Review
Rabbi Ezra Bloch
Rabbi Doniel Manevich
Rabbi Chaim Pinchos Miller
Rabbi Pinchas Rabinovicz

Educational Consultants
Rabbi Shalom Strajcher
Rabbi Aryeh Belsky
Rabbi Yaakov Yosef Batelman
Rabbi Shalom Einhorn
Mr. Richard Altabee

Grade Level Consultant
Mrs. Rivkie Levovitz

Proofreading
Mrs. Rochelle Gemal
Mrs. Liba Grant
Mrs. Miriam Hirsch
Mrs. Chaya Hoberman

Teacher Resources

Director
Mrs. Chani Wilhelm

Project Coordinators
Mrs. Chaya Aliza Deckelbaum
Mrs. Aydel Stein

Editors
Rabbi Beryl Schiff
Rabbi Nosson Klugman

Curriculum Support
Mrs. Esther Blitz

Technical Staff

Project Coordinators
Mrs. Judy Wax
Mrs. Faige Shoshana

Book Design
Mr. Yanky Goldman / Papermasters

Art Director / Illustrator
Mr. Shepsil Scheinberg

Graphics and Typesetting
Mrs. Bassie Gutman
Mrs. Tova Rivka Sasson
Chaya Ruti Weintraub
Mr. Naftali Miller

Executive Committee

Chairman
Rabbi Elyakim Walkin

Vice President of Planning and Development
Mr. Sheldon Fliegelman

Material for this textbook was selected and adapted from the "Encyclopedia of the Taryag Mitzvoth" by Mrs. Ahuva Weiss, Rabbi Shimon Finkelman, and Rabbi Moishe Bak

Acknowledgments

Rabbinical Advisers
Rabbi Yisroel Belsky, shlita
Rabbi Reuven Feinstein, shlita

Research
Rabbi Naftali Erlanger, *Director*

Rabbi Mordechai Aronofsky
Rabbi Yosef Gavriel Bechhofer
Rabbi Nochum Brown
Rabbi Moshe Eisemann
Rabbi Yisroel Eliach
Rabbi Avrohom Erlanger
Rabbi Yitzchok Erlanger
Rabbi Yitzchok Freund
Rabbi Zev Freund
Rabbi Yehudah Herschler
Rabbi Yeshayahu Levy
Rabbi Shaul Lieberman
Rabbi Ari Lobel
Rabbi Saar Meizel
Rabbi Yitzchok Rosenblum
Rabbi Ariel Schweitzer
Rabbi Moshe Tikochinsky
Yeshiva Ohr HaDaas

Educational Contributors
Rabbi Binyomin Ginsberg
Rabbi Hillel Mandel
Rabbi Mechel Rottenberg
Rebbetzin Shelia Feinstein
Mrs. Shulamis May
Mrs. Rifka Rosman

U.S. Educational Office
Mrs. Estie Ginsburg
Mrs. Nechama Kahanow
Bashie Salamon
Sora Zimmerman

Jerusalem Educational Office
Rabbi Shmuel Elyashiv, *Director*
Mrs. Shevi Reiman
Mrs. Leah Eisenstein

Photo Credits
Vilna Gaon photo, CIS Publishers

We offer our sincere thanks to the Foundation for the Jewish Community, a Foundation of Donor Advised Funds, whose donors and staff helped make this work possible. FJC's donors support many worthy causes, not only through their grants, but with their mission-based investing. Financing from FJC's Agency Loan Fund was critical in bringing our efforts to fruition.

Their decision to support this project came at a turning point in our work. Multitudes yet unborn will be indebted to FJC's donors, who had the vision to utilize FJC to manage their charitable funds. (FJC, the premier foundation of donor advised funds for discerning philanthropists, is a public charity that provides total management of charitable giving. To learn more about how you can participate in supporting other worthy projects, call 888-GIVE-FJC or visit www.fjc.org.)

We are most grateful to the Kushner Foundation for their vision and support of this ambitious and monumental undertaking.

Table of Contents

About the Textbook

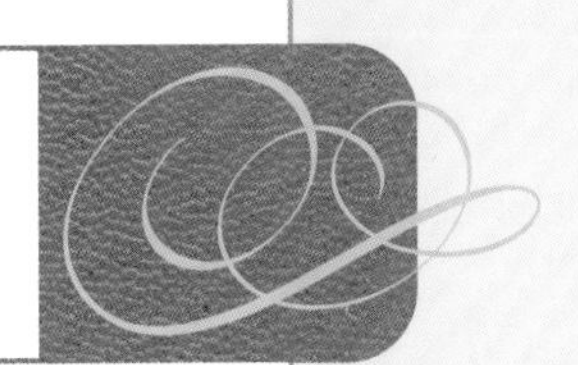

Dear Student,

Welcome to the Taryag Legacy Foundation's Taryag Mitzah Project. You are about to embark on an amazing journey: the journey to learn and master the תרי"ג מצוות. This textbook will be your guide, together with your Rebbi or Morah, on the wondrous journey ahead.

The material found in the textbook is based on the information found in the *Encyclopedia of the Taryag Mitzvoth*, although original sources are cited after the relevant paragraphs as well.

As you look through your textbook you will see that each mitzvah is divided into different sections. Each section is designed to help you learn the mitzvah and understand it to the best of your ability. A short description of each section is found below.

The Mitzvah

At the beginning of each mitzvah, you will see a box toward the left-hand side of the page. This box contains a short definition of the mitzvah. Underneath that box, at the bottom of the page, you will find important **KEYWORDS**. These words are found within the unit and will be explained by your teacher. They will help you to understand the material better. They will also be used in the workbook pages, as well as in the Comprehensive Assessment for each mitzvah.

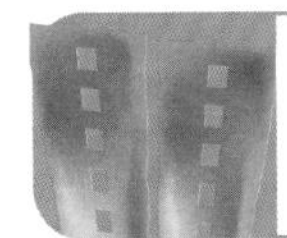

Introduction to the Mitzvah — SECTION I

On the page opposite **The Mitzvah**, you will find an introduction to each mitzvah. Included in this section will be an explanation of the mitzvah, as well as other concepts and explanations brought down by the Gemara or other commentaries.

The Source of the Mitzvah — SECTION II

This section tells you where in the Torah you can find the commandment for this mitzvah and the exact words of the פסוק. It also gives you a paragraph or two dealing with the Torah's words on the mitzvah.

The Laws of the Mitzvah

This section gives a brief summary of laws pertaining to the mitzvah. The הלכות found here are in no way complete, but they offer major points. Further study can be done using the *Encyclopedia of the Taryag Mitzvoth*, and any of the other commentaries on the תרי״ג מצוות.

טוב טעם
Appreciating the Mitzvah

This section is full of additional insights and possible reasons for the mitzvah. It may also include stories and מְשָׁלִים, *parables*, from Tanach, Mishnah, Gemara, Rishonim, and other commentaries.

Living the Mitzvah

This section contains a story pertaining to the mitzvah. The material can be a novelization of a story from Tanach, a dramatization of a story or incident in the Gemara, or a story about a Rishon or Acharon. These stories are not only for your enjoyment, but they also bring out different aspects of the mitzvah itself and important lessons to be learned. Every story is accompanied by beautifully crafted illustrations, making the story not only more pleasurable to read, but also more understandable and memorable.

It must be noted that the stories included in the student textbook are just that — stories. Although many of them draw upon sources in Tanach, Medrashim, and the Gemara, thematic material has been added to create story lines that will be engaging to the student. The sources upon which each story has been based can be found in the Teacher's Edition.

Expand Your Knowledge

This section does exactly what it says; it expands your knowledge of the mitzvah. This section can contain interesting situations and what the halachah would be regarding the mitzvah. It can also give a more in depth look at some of the מצוות. This section may be a little more difficult than the other sections, but it will also be interesting.

Determine Mastery

At the end of each mitzvah unit you will find a list of review questions designed to ensure that you understood all the reading material. Each mitzvah also contains at least one question that involves **Critical Thinking** to see if you can apply what you have learned. Sometimes a challenge question will be presented under the heading of **Investigate and Inquire.** This question will involve some kind of research on your part, and should prove exciting and fun.

Throughout the sections are **Think & Share** questions that are designed to enable you to think and discuss the topics with your teacher and classmates. There are also little paragraphs on the sidebars of some of the pages that contain bits of information of which you might not have been aware. You should find these **Did You Know** boxes very informative. **Focus** questions and **Reading Checks** are provided after some paragraphs to ensure that you have understood what you read.

The **Glossary** offers you definitions and explanations of words you might find difficult to understand. The glossary is in alphabetical order and is easy to use.

Finally, a word about the Hebrew text found in the textbook. When quoting פסוקים, or using a word that is not common or is new to you, the textbook offers words with ניקוד, *vowelization*. However, there are many words which you will recognize by sight, and these will have no vowelization. However, in order to help you read these words without נקודות, they will sometimes have an extra ו' or י' in places to make them easier to read; for example, the word אסור, *prohibition*, will be written as איסור. This is called כתיב מלא.

This textbook, together with the additional student resources, such as the Student Workbook and the Mitzvah Cards, will give you the ability to become a Mitzvah Master. You and your classmates, guided by your Rebbi or Morah, will learn each mitzvah in depth, and will know how to keep these מצוות to the best of your knowledge and ability.

We hope you are ready, because your תרי"ג מצוות ship is about to set sail. Turn the page, and let your journey begin!

Introduction

Introduction

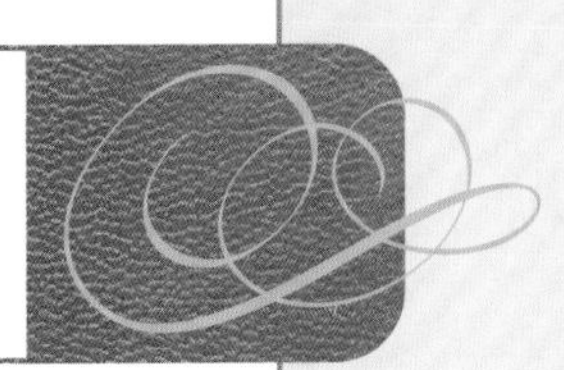

וְעָשִׂיתָ אֶת כָּל מִצְוֹתָיו אֲשֶׁר אָנֹכִי מְצַוְּךָ הַיּוֹם (דברים ל:ח)

What is a mitzvah? We all know the answer to that question. A mitzvah is a commandment. We also know that there are two kinds of מצוות, a positive commandment, an עשה, and a negative commandment, a לא תעשה. The positive commandments are ones that require an action, thought, or belief on our part, such as building a *succah* on סוכות and reciting *kiddush* on שבת. Negative commandments are ones that require us to abstain from doing an action or thinking a thought or belief, such as not doing any *melachah* on שבת and not worshipping עבודה זרה. Hashem gave us תרי״ג, six hundred and thirteen, מצוות; two hundred and forty-eight מצוות עשה and three hundred and sixty-five מצוות לא תעשה.

Why do we keep the מצוות? We know the answer to that question as well. We keep the מצוות because Hashem commanded us to keep them. The commentaries may give possible reasons for the מצוות. However, these reasons are secondary, to help us understand the מצוות more fully so that we can observe them more completely. We must always remember that we should be keeping the מצוות because we said נעשה ונשמע on Har Sinai over three thousand years ago!

Did you know that every נשמה was present at מתן תורה? Over three million people were standing at the foot of the mountain, while around them were all the נשמות that would ever be born. Together, they all received Hashem's Torah on Har Sinai. We know this to be true. We know that Hashem gave us the Torah because the story has been passed down from father to son, from mother to daughter, from that day until this one. And with each telling, the story stays the same. There is no exaggeration, there are no differences. The record of that story is the same today as it was on the sixth day of Sivan, 2448.

Let us look back now to that glorious day when Hashem gave us, His Chosen People, the Torah, His most treasured gift…

וַיִּחַן שָׁם יִשְׂרָאֵל נֶגֶד הָהָר

Bnei Yisrael were camped at the foot of Har Sinai, like one man, with one heart, eagerly awaiting Hashem's instructions.

Hashem told Moshe, "The reason I have brought you (Bnei Yisrael) to Har Sinai is so that you should serve Me … If you keep My covenant … you are ready to receive My Torah and to become My Chosen People. You alone will be beloved by Me. Although the whole earth is Mine, I will cherish only you from among all the nations. You shall be unto Me a ממלכת כהנים, *a kingdom of Kohanim,* and a גוי קדוש, *a holy nation.*" Hashem also told Moshe that He would appear in a thick cloud, and all the people would hear when Hashem spoke to Moshe.

Moshe returned to the people and related to them Hashem's words. All of Bnei Yisrael were willing to accept the Torah. They answered with one voice: כל אשר דבר ה׳ נעשה ונשמע, *All that Hashem has said, we will do, and we will hear.*

But Bnei Yisrael had one request: They longed to hear Hashem Himself, and receive the Torah directly from Him.

Hashem agreed to Bnei Yisrael's request, and told Moshe to tell the people to prepare for מתן תורה.

For three days, Bnei Yisrael prepared themselves. They immersed themselves in the מקוה, they washed their clothes, and they cleansed themselves spiritually as well. Hashem healed all their physical defects. At the end of their preparations, the people were like angels. Indeed, Bnei Yisrael had reached the level of אדם הראשון before he sinned. They were ready to receive the Torah.

It was שבת morning, the sixth of Sivan. Har Sinai was trembling with excitement. Bnei Yisrael were awakened by thunder, lightning, and the sound of the shofar. Moshe called to them, "The חתן is waiting to greet His כלה."

All of Bnei Yisrael, men, women, and children, assembled at the foot of Har Sinai. There they were joined by all the unborn souls of their descendants, and by the souls of all the גרים who would accept the Torah in future generations.

In an awe-inspiring display of thunder, lightning, smoke, shofar blasts, and fire, Hashem's Presence descended on Har Sinai, surrounded by twenty-two thousand angels. The shofar became continuously louder, building in intensity, until it reached the highest volume that people could hear. The fire rose up to the very heavens. The mountain smoked like a furnace. The people trembled with fear. And the whole world was quiet. Not a creature stirred; the birds did not fly, the cows did not moo, the oceans were still, the angels stopped saying *shirah.*

As Hashem began to speak, the people not only heard His voice, but saw the sound waves as well. As each commandment was said, the words themselves traveled as a fiery wave around the entire מחנה and approached each Jew individually, asking, "Do you accept upon yourself this commandment, and all the הלכות, *laws,* pertaining to it?" Every single Jew answered, "Yes." The fire then engraved itself upon the לוחות.

Hashem first stated all the דברות together, at the same time. Then He began to recite each one individually. Each person did not experience the full impact of Hashem's voice. Rather, each individual perceived it according to his capacity to experience the שכינה, *the Divine Presence*. Even so, as Hashem declared, "אָנֹכִי ה' אֱלֹקֶיךָ," the realization of Hashem's Presence was too much for them to bear, and their souls left their bodies.

Hashem brought them all back to life, and even filled the air with spicy fragrances to revive them from the shock. But as Hashem said the second דברה, "לֹא יִהְיֶה לְךָ אֱלֹהִים אֲחֵרִים," the same thing happened again.

After the first two commandments, Bnei Yisrael could not stand it any more. They begged Moshe to tell them the rest of the דברות. They could not bear to hear Hashem's voice again. Moshe recited the other eight commandments, and Hashem amplified his voice so everyone could hear him.

Each commandment is in singular form so that no Jew can say, "It's all right if I don't do this mitzvah, because everyone else is doing it." Each Jew is obligated to keep each mitzvah. And we do. From that day on, Bnei Yisrael have been keeping the מצוות, living a Torah way of life. From the sixth day of Sivan, 2448, until this very day, we have kept the מצוות. And we will continue to keep the מצוות each and every day.

As you begin to learn the תרי"ג מצוות, you will strengthen your recognition of the מצוות by delving into what it is Hashem really wants us to accomplish. Today begins your journey; a journey that began over three thousand years ago in the desert, at the foot of a small, inconsequential mountain. As you learn each mitzvah in depth, you will place your footsteps next to those that have been imprinted throughout the ages. You will understand each mitzvah better, so that you can perform it to the best of your ability. This is a journey that your parents, Rabbeim, and מורות have prepared you for all your life. This is your legacy.

THE SINGER EDITION

ספר
עשרת הדברות

ללמוד • לשמור • לעשות

THE MITZVOTH OF THE ASERETH HADIBROTH

MITZVAH 25
MITZVAH 26
MITZVAH 27
MITZVAH 28
MITZVAH 29
MITZVAH 30
MITZVAH 31
MITZVAH 32
MITZVAH 33
MITZVAH 34
MITZVAH 35
MITZVAH 36
MITZVAH 37
MITZVAH 38

Dedicated by

Jonah and Jo Bruck and Family
Chicago, Illinois

מצוה

MITZVAH

25

Believe in the Existence of Hashem

מצות האמונה בשם יתברך

MITZVAH **25**

מצות האמונה בשם יתברך

Believe in the Existence of Hashem

THE MITZVAH

A person is obligated to know that there is a God Who brought everything into existence and continuously sustains it all. We must also know that this God, Whom we refer to as Hashem, is the all-powerful Master of the universe and He directs and controls all that happens with His limitless power.

- עִקָּרִים
- בּוֹרֵא
- מַנְהִיג
- שֶׁיִּתְמַהְמֵהַּ
- דורות
- יֵשׁ מֵאַיִן
- תְּמִידִיּוֹת
- עֲשָׂרָה נִסְיוֹנוֹת

SECTION I

Introduction to the Mitzvah

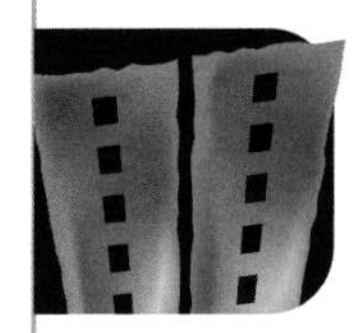

If you think back to your earliest memories, you have always known that Hashem is the Creator and Master of all. You knew, even when you were a small child, that Hashem makes all things happen, like the sun rising and setting each day.

You knew because of our *mesorah,* the chain that connects us to the past. Your parents taught you *emunah* the same way their parents taught them, all the way back to our forefather, Avraham.

Chazal tell us that when Avraham Avinu was very small, he had to hide from the wicked king, Nimrod. Nimrod wanted to kill him because his astrologers foresaw that Avraham and his descendants would conquer many kings, including Nimrod himself. While hiding in a cave, Avraham explored and questioned the workings of the universe, until he realized the truth: There is only One Being Who created everything, there is no other, and this One Being sustains everything He created.

Once Avraham understood this, he went to find someone to teach him Hashem's ways. So he went to learn from Noach and Shem. Noach, together with his son, Shem, lived a life that followed Hashem's ways. They were both survivors of the great *Mabbul.* They had received an unbroken *mesorah* that went straight back to אדם הראשון. Avraham Avinu knew that in order to learn how to serve Hashem properly, he had to restore that *mesorah* and pass it on to future דורות, *generations.*

Later on, Avraham, together with his wife, Sarah, taught their belief in Hashem to others, until there were tens of thousands of people who believed in Hashem.

Most importantly, Avraham taught his beliefs to his son, Yitzchak, who taught them to his son, Yaakov, and so on, down through the ages, until today.

Think & Share

Why is our mesorah so important to our emunah?

Avraham Avinu taught us that *emunah* in Hashem is to know and be aware that there is a Supreme Being Who created all that exists; that He created the universe from nothing (יֵשׁ מֵאַיִן); and that nothing can survive without Hashem's continued הַשְׁגָּחָה.

~ see *Rambam,* הלכות עבודת כוכבים ch. 1

The Source of the Mitzvah

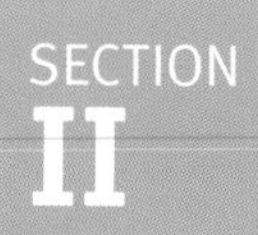

אָנֹכִי ה' אֱלֹקֶיךָ אֲשֶׁר הוֹצֵאתִיךָ מֵאֶרֶץ מִצְרַיִם

שמות כ:ב פרשת יתרו

I am Hashem, your God, Who has taken you out of the land of Egypt

The פסוק states, אָנֹכִי ה' אֱלֹקֶיךָ אֲשֶׁר הוֹצֵאתִיךָ מֵאֶרֶץ מִצְרַיִם, *I am Hashem, your God, Who has taken you out of the land of Egypt.* Some Rishonim comment that the words אֲשֶׁר הוֹצֵאתִיךָ מֵאֶרֶץ מִצְרַיִם not only identify who Hashem is — the One Who took us out of Mitzrayim — but are also part of the mitzvah. We are not only required to know that Hashem exists, but we must also know that Hashem miraculously redeemed us from Mitzrayim.

This teaches us that everything in the universe is under Hashem's control. Hashem can even suspend the laws of nature, since it was He Who created those laws in the first place. This was clearly demonstrated in Mitzrayim, from the ten מכות through the splitting of the ים סוף, which were all clearly not natural occurrences, but rather miracles performed on our behalf by Hashem.

~ *Sefer HaChinuch* §25

Furthermore, some Rishonim add that since these words are the opening words of the עשרת הדברות, this mitzvah also requires us to know that Hashem gave us the Torah.

~ see דרשות הר"ן §9

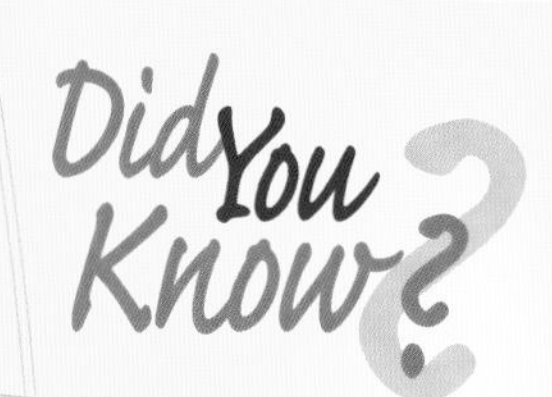

The פסוק states אנכי ה' אלקיך, I am Hashem, "your" God, and not I am Hashem, "the" God. This teaches us that we are obligated not only to believe that Hashem is the Lord of the universe, but also to believe that He supervises and guides each individual being at all times (הַשְׁגָּחָה פְּרָטִית).

~ *Sefer HaIkkarim* 3:18

Reading Check

What lesson in emunah do we learn from the miracles that Hashem performed for us in Mitzrayim?

A person is obligated to know that there is a God Who brought everything into existence and continuously sustains it all. We must also know that this God, Whom we refer to as Hashem, is the all-powerful Master of the universe and He directs and controls all that happens with His limitless power.

The Laws of the Mitzvah

1. A person fulfills this mitzvah by believing that there is a God Who created everything, continually sustains all He created, and Whose powers are unlimited. We must also believe that:

a. Hashem always existed and will always exist, and that before the creation of the world, nothing existed except Hashem.

b. Everything is dependent upon Hashem for its continued existence, but Hashem is not dependent upon anything.

c. Hashem has no body and no form.

2. This mitzvah is one of the six constant מצוות (שֵׁשׁ מִצְווֹת תְּמִידִיּוֹת). A person is obligated in these six מצוות every moment of his entire life, and is rewarded each moment that he thinks about them.

3. A person fulfills this mitzvah by believing that the above concepts are true, even though he does not understand why they are true. However, it is praiseworthy for a person to constantly try to deepen his awareness and understanding of Hashem's existence.

4. This mitzvah applies to both men and women, in all places and at all times.

5. One who does not believe in Hashem excludes himself from the nation of Yisrael, is called a heretic (מִין), and has no portion in עולם הבא.

Note: For the prohibition to believe in other gods, see Mitzvah 26. For the mitzvah to know that Hashem is One, see Mitzvah 417.

טוב טעם
Appreciating the Mitzvah

The Foundation of the Torah

The mitzvah of *emunah* is not simply a separate commandment, rather *emunah* serves as the foundation of the entire Torah. When a person believes in a Creator Who not only created everything, but continues to manage and sustain everything, that person will feel that it is his duty to fulfill the will of that Creator, to Whom he owes his entire existence. This is what the words of the first of the עשרת הדברות come to teach us. אנכי ה׳, *I am Hashem,* is teaching us that we must recognize Hashem's existence and the fact that He granted us life and all that we have. This concept should be clear to us at all times. אלקיך, *your God,* teaches us that we should accept Hashem as our God and devote ourselves to serving Him.

~ *Mefaresh* to the *Rambam,* הלכות יסודי התורה ch.1

With the words of the first commandment, Hashem is also telling us that He is our God, our Creator, our Lawgiver, our Judge. Everything we have, every breath we take, is granted to us by Hashem. Hashem wants us to look upon ourselves as His property and be the instrument of His will. He wants us to join His choir of creation as His servants, His creatures.

~ *R' Samson Raphael Hirsch, Chorev,* תורות 1:4

The מצוות Are the Key to Our *Emunah*

Every time we perform a mitzvah or study Torah, we are strengthening our *emunah.* When a person performs a mitzvah for no reason other than his belief in Hashem and His Torah, it deepens his faith in Hashem.

~ *Yismach Moshe,* פרשת תרומה

Every time we do a mitzvah, we are also fulfilling the mitzvah of *emunah* in Hashem as well.

This is not only true when we perform a mitzvah or refrain from doing an *aveirah.* A person fulfills the mitzvah of *emunah* in Hashem just by thinking about doing a mitzvah or pushing away a forbidden thought, as long as he does so out of awareness of Hashem and His Torah.

~ *Degel Machaneh Ephraim,* פרשת בראשית ד"ה או

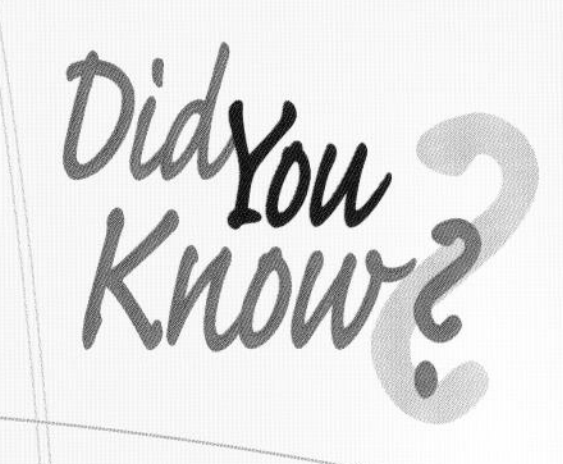

Part of the mitzvah of emunah is the belief that Hashem has no body or form. Yet, throughout Tanach, we find references to Hashem's physical attributes, such as יָד חֲזָקָה, a strong hand, אֶצְבַּע אֱלֹקִים, the finger of God, עֵינֵי ה׳, the eyes of Hashem, and אָזְנֵי ה׳, the ears of Hashem. The Torah uses these expressions only to make it easier for a human being to understand.

~ *Rambam,* הלכות יסודי התורה 1:8-9

A person is obligated to know that there is a God Who brought everything into existence and continuously sustains it all. We must also know that this God, Whom we refer to as Hashem, is the all-powerful Master of the universe and He directs and controls all that happens with His limitless power.

Chazal tell us (אבות 2:1): הֱוֵי זָהִיר בְּמִצְוָה קַלָּה כְּבַחֲמוּרָה, *Be as scrupulous with a minor mitzvah as with a major one.* Every mitzvah is to be treasured because, with each one, a person recognizes Hashem, and the ultimate purpose of all the מצוות is that we come to believe in Hashem and give thanks to Him for creating us.

~ see *Ramban,* שמות 13:16

The Strength to Die על קידוש השם

The strength to give up our lives for our belief in Hashem was planted forever, deep within us, when Hashem declared, "אָנֹכִי ה' אֱלֹקֶיךָ, *I am Hashem, your God.*" When those who were standing at Har Sinai heard this declaration, it became second nature to them to believe in its truth.

~ *Derech Pikudecha,* מצוות עשה §25; *Pri Tzaddik, Rosh Hashanah* §15

This *middah* of being willing to give up our lives for our belief in Hashem is a part of each and every one of us. When Nimrod threw Avraham into the כִּבְשַׁן הָאֵשׁ, Avraham was ready to die עַל קִדּוּשׁ ה'. We in turn inherited this characteristic from our forefather, Avraham. This is why, says R' Chaim of Volozhin, when the Mishnah in פרקי אבות (5:3) enumerates the עֲשָׂרָה נִסְיוֹנוֹת, the *ten tests* of Avraham, he is called Avinu, *our father.* For just as we inherited different genes and characteristics from our mother and father, so too did Bnei Yisrael inherit certain מִדּוֹת from our father, Avraham.

~ see *Ruach Chaim* to אבות 5:3

The Six Constant מצוות

There are six מצוות (see *More on the Mitzvah* at right) which we are obligated to keep at all times. These מצוות do not require any action, just thought and constant awareness. They are not dependent upon a particular time — as is the mitzvah to live in a *succah* on סוכות — or a specific situation — as is the mitzvah to pay a worker his wages the same day he works for you. Every moment of our lives, these מצוות should be in our minds.

~ *Biur Halachah* 1:1 ד"ה הוא כלל, citing *Hakdamah* to *Sefer HaChinuch*

שש מצוות תמידיות

Mitzvah 25: To know that Hashem exists

Mitzvah 26: Not to believe that another god exists aside from Hashem

Mitzvah 417: To know that Hashem is One

Mitzvah 418: To love Hashem

Mitzvah 432: To fear Hashem

Mitzvah 387: Not to be led astray by our thoughts or by what we see

Living the Mitzvah

The Best Purchase

Unkelos, the son of Kelonimus, was the nephew of the all powerful Caesar, the emperor who ruled much of the world, including Eretz Yisrael. He lived during the time following חֻרְבַּן בַּית שֵׁנִי, when Rome possessed great power and wealth.

But Unkelos wanted none of that. He was not interested in money or fame. Art, music, and philosophy held no appeal for him. He began to study religion, but the Roman mythology left him with an empty feeling. He wanted to study Torah.

Through the study of Torah, Unkelos recognized the truth. He understood that Hashem is the Creator Who brought all things into being; and that no creation can survive without the continued supply of His sustenance. Unkelos realized that the Torah is true, and that he should follow Hashem's commandments.

Unkelos wanted to be a Jew. However, conversion to Judaism was against Roman law, and was punishable by death. How could he, the nephew of the emperor, convert and actually live as a Jew?

He went to his uncle and said, "Great Caesar, I seek your advice. I wish to become a merchant, to go out into the world and make my fortune. How should I proceed?"

Caesar was happy that his nephew, whom he loved, was showing some ambition.

A person is obligated to know that there is a God Who brought everything into existence and continuously sustains it all. We must also know that this God, Whom we refer to as Hashem, is the all-powerful Master of the universe and He directs and controls all that happens with His limitless power.

He told him, "Find something that no one finds useful. You will not have to pay a lot for it. It will eventually increase in value, and you will then be able to sell it for a high price."

Unkelos thanked the emperor for his advice and immediately traveled to Yerushalayim, where he became a Jew and devoted his life to learning Torah day and night.

As time passed, the emperor missed his nephew and began to wonder what had become of him. He sent messengers to seek out Unkelos. When the emperor learned where his nephew was and what he was doing, he was shocked. "How can this be?" he raged. "Has my nephew lost his mind? A noble Roman wanting to be a lowly Jew? What a disgrace!"

Caesar sent a contingent of officers to his nephew to convince him of the error of his ways, and bring him back to Rome.

When the soldiers approached Unkelos, he spoke to them with warmth and wisdom. "Why serve the king of Rome," Unkelos asked them, "when you can serve the King of the entire universe, the King Who created Caesar himself?" The soldiers were enchanted, and longed to hear more. All of them remained with Unkelos and converted to Judaism as well.

The emperor was not at all happy when he found out what had happened. He ordered a second garrison of soldiers to go and bring back his nephew, but he warned them not to allow Unkelos to engage them in conversation. "Do not answer him when he speaks to you!" commanded the king. But Unkelos had the same effect on the second group as well.

"When an army travels at night," he told them, "the lower-ranking soldiers hold the torches for the higher-ranking soldiers, and the higher-ranking soldiers hold the torches for those who outrank them, and so on, up until the generals themselves light the way for Caesar. But does Caesar hold a torch for anyone?"

The soldiers shrugged and shook their heads, not understanding the point Unkelos was trying to make.

"Well," continued Unkelos, "the King of the universe lit the way for the Jews with pillars of fire as they wandered in the desert for forty years. The King of the universe takes care of us; we do not need to take care of Him."

The soldiers were enthralled and wanted to hear more. They too remained and converted to Judaism.

When this garrison also failed to return to Rome, Caesar decided he had had enough. He sent a final unit of soldiers, with orders to bring Unkelos back, no matter what.

The soldiers marched into Unkelos' house, lifted Unkelos off his feet, and began to carry him out. As they reached the doorway, Unkelos managed to reach out and touch the *mezuzah*.

A person is obligated to know that there is a God Who brought everything into existence and continuously sustains it all. We must also know that this God, Whom we refer to as Hashem, is the all-powerful Master of the universe and He directs and controls all that happens with His limitless power.

The soldiers stopped and looked at one another. They all wondered at this strange action. So they asked Unkelos, "What did you just do? What was that you just touched?"

Unkelos explained, "In Rome, the Caesar sits in his palace, far from his people, surrounded by guards who protect him from harm. But our King, the King of the universe, is different. As we Jews sit in our houses, He comes to us and protects us, as a father watches over his children. We put a *mezuzah* on each of our doors, for Hashem is watching over us."

These guards also remained and converted.

Caesar finally admitted defeat and sent his nephew a letter asking him to come to Rome, and promising that no harm would befall him.

Unkelos accepted the invitation. When he arrived and was presented before the emperor, Caesar had only one question for him: Why?

"I took your advice," Unkelos replied. "I looked around the world and found one thing that no one values — Judaism — and I purchased it for myself. I know that one day, when משיח arrives, the Jewish people will be the most precious commodity in the world. There is no better business venture than to become a Jew, a member of Hashem's special nation.

Unkelos spent the rest of his life learning Torah. Some Meforshim say that he was the same Unkelos who wrote Targum Unkelos on the Torah. Unkelos became a great *tzaddik* and תלמיד חכם.

What gave Unkelos the strength to leave a life of honor and wealth, and withstand the pressures of his uncle, so that he could become a Jew?

Expand Your Knowledge

THE THIRTEEN PRINCIPLES
שלשה עשר עיקרים

There is a difference of opinion among the authorities as to how many basic beliefs are commanded to us by the Torah. The generally accepted number of these core beliefs is thirteen, as enumerated by the Rambam.

It is a praiseworthy practice to recite these Thirteen Principles of Faith every day. In fact, the Rambam writes that a person must constantly review and study them so that they become part of his way of thinking, and he must always bear them in mind.

Many people recite a shortened version of these Thirteen Principles, the "Ani Maamins," at the end of שחרית*. Some people recite the* תפילה *of* יגדל *every morning, which is also a summary of Rambam's principles.*

On the following pages, you will find the Thirteen Principles of the Rambam, the corresponding Ani Maamim and stanza in יגדל*, and the English translation of the Ani Maamin.*

Principle #1

Belief in the existence of Hashem

אֲנִי מַאֲמִין בֶּאֱמוּנָה שְׁלֵמָה, שֶׁהַבּוֹרֵא יִתְבָּרַךְ שְׁמוֹ הוּא בּוֹרֵא וּמַנְהִיג לְכָל הַבְּרוּאִים, וְהוּא לְבַדּוֹ עָשָׂה וְעוֹשֶׂה וְיַעֲשֶׂה לְכָל הַמַּעֲשִׂים.

I believe with complete faith that the Creator, Blessed is His Name, creates and guides all creations, and that He alone has made, makes, and will make all things.

יִגְדַּל אֱלֹהִים חַי וְיִשְׁתַּבַּח, נִמְצָא, וְאֵין עֵת אֶל מְצִיאוּתוֹ.

Principle #2

Belief that Hashem is One

אֲנִי מַאֲמִין בֶּאֱמוּנָה שְׁלֵמָה, שֶׁהַבּוֹרֵא יִתְבָּרַךְ שְׁמוֹ הוּא יָחִיד, וְאֵין יְחִידוּת כָּמוֹהוּ בְּשׁוּם פָּנִים, וְהוּא לְבַדּוֹ אֱלֹקֵינוּ, הָיָה הֹוֶה וְיִהְיֶה.

I believe with complete faith that the Creator, Blessed is His Name, is One and there is no one else who is One like Him in any way, and He alone is our God — He was, He is, and He will always be.

אֶחָד וְאֵין יָחִיד כְּיִחוּדוֹ, נֶעְלָם, וְגַם אֵין סוֹף לְאַחְדּוּתוֹ.

Principle #3

Belief that Hashem has no body or form

אֲנִי מַאֲמִין בֶּאֱמוּנָה שְׁלֵמָה, שֶׁהַבּוֹרֵא יִתְבָּרַךְ שְׁמוֹ אֵינוֹ גוּף, וְלֹא יַשִּׂיגוּהוּ מַשִּׂיגֵי הַגּוּף, וְאֵין לוֹ שׁוּם דִּמְיוֹן כְּלָל.

I believe with complete faith that the Creator, Blessed is His Name, has no physical body and physical concepts do not apply to Him, and there is nothing that can compare to Him at all.

אֵין לוֹ דְּמוּת הַגּוּף וְאֵינוֹ גוּף, לֹא נַעֲרוֹךְ אֵלָיו קְדֻשָּׁתוֹ.

Principle #4

Belief that Hashem is eternal. He existed before anything else and will exist after everything else

אֲנִי מַאֲמִין בֶּאֱמוּנָה שְׁלֵמָה, שֶׁהַבּוֹרֵא יִתְבָּרַךְ שְׁמוֹ הוּא רִאשׁוֹן וְהוּא אַחֲרוֹן.

I believe with complete faith that the Creator, Blessed is His Name, is the first and the last.

קַדְמוֹן לְכָל דָּבָר אֲשֶׁר נִבְרָא, רִאשׁוֹן וְאֵין רֵאשִׁית לְרֵאשִׁיתוֹ.

Principle #5

Belief that Hashem is the only One Whom it is proper to pray to and serve

אֲנִי מַאֲמִין בֶּאֱמוּנָה שְׁלֵמָה, שֶׁהַבּוֹרֵא יִתְבָּרַךְ שְׁמוֹ לוֹ לְבַדּוֹ רָאוּי לְהִתְפַּלֵּל, וְאֵין לְזוּלָתוֹ רָאוּי לְהִתְפַּלֵּל.

I believe with complete faith that the Creator, Blessed is His Name, is the only One to Whom it is proper to pray, and it is not proper to pray to any other.

הִנּוֹ אֲדוֹן עוֹלָם לְכָל נוֹצָר, יוֹרֶה גְדֻלָּתוֹ וּמַלְכוּתוֹ.

Principle #6

Belief that Hashem communicates to mankind through נביאים

אֲנִי מַאֲמִין בֶּאֱמוּנָה שְׁלֵמָה, שֶׁכָּל דִּבְרֵי נְבִיאִים אֱמֶת.

I believe with complete faith that all the words of the נביאים are true.

שֶׁפַע נְבוּאָתוֹ נְתָנוֹ, אֶל אַנְשֵׁי סְגֻלָּתוֹ וְתִפְאַרְתּוֹ.

Principle #7

Belief that Moshe Rabbeinu was the greatest נביא

אֲנִי מַאֲמִין בֶּאֱמוּנָה שְׁלֵמָה, שֶׁנְּבוּאַת מֹשֶׁה רַבֵּנוּ עָלָיו הַשָּׁלוֹם הָיְתָה אֲמִתִּית, וְשֶׁהוּא הָיָה אָב לַנְּבִיאִים, לַקּוֹדְמִים לְפָנָיו וְלַבָּאִים אַחֲרָיו.

I believe with complete faith that the prophecy of Moshe Rabbeinu, may peace be upon him, was true and that he was the greatest of נביאים, of those who came before him and of those who came after him.

לֹא קָם בְּיִשְׂרָאֵל כְּמֹשֶׁה עוֹד, נָבִיא וּמַבִּיט אֶת תְּמוּנָתוֹ.

*Principle #**8***

Belief that the entire Torah we now possess is the one that Moshe received from Hashem

אֲנִי מַאֲמִין בֶּאֱמוּנָה שְׁלֵמָה, שֶׁכָּל הַתּוֹרָה הַמְּצוּיָה עַתָּה
בְּיָדֵינוּ, הִיא הַנְּתוּנָה לְמֹשֶׁה רַבֵּנוּ עָלָיו הַשָּׁלוֹם.

I believe with complete faith that the entire Torah that is now in our possession is the same Torah that was given to Moshe Rabbeinu, may peace be upon him.

תּוֹרַת אֱמֶת נָתַן לְעַמּוֹ קֵל, עַל יַד נְבִיאוֹ נֶאֱמַן בֵּיתוֹ.

*Principle #**9***

Belief that the Torah is Hashem's permanent word and it will not and cannot be changed

אֲנִי מַאֲמִין בֶּאֱמוּנָה שְׁלֵמָה, שֶׁזֹּאת הַתּוֹרָה לֹא תְהֵא מֻחְלֶפֶת,
וְלֹא תְהֵא תּוֹרָה אַחֶרֶת מֵאֵת הַבּוֹרֵא יִתְבָּרַךְ שְׁמוֹ.

I believe with complete faith that this Torah will not be exchanged for another, and there will not be another Torah from the Creator, Blessed is His Name.

לֹא יַחֲלִיף הָקֵל וְלֹא יָמִיר דָּתוֹ, לְעוֹלָמִים, לְזוּלָתוֹ.

*Principle #**10***

Belief that Hashem knows all men's actions and thoughts

אֲנִי מַאֲמִין בֶּאֱמוּנָה שְׁלֵמָה, שֶׁהַבּוֹרֵא יִתְבָּרַךְ שְׁמוֹ יוֹדֵעַ
כָּל מַעֲשֵׂה בְנֵי אָדָם וְכָל מַחְשְׁבוֹתָם, שֶׁנֶּאֱמַר, הַיֹּצֵר יַחַד
לִבָּם, הַמֵּבִין אֶל כָּל מַעֲשֵׂיהֶם.

I believe with complete faith that the Creator, Blessed is His Name, knows all the deeds of human beings and their thoughts, as it is said, "He Who forms their hearts all together, He Who understands all their deeds."

צוֹפֶה וְיוֹדֵעַ סְתָרֵינוּ, מַבִּיט לְסוֹף דָּבָר בְּקַדְמָתוֹ.

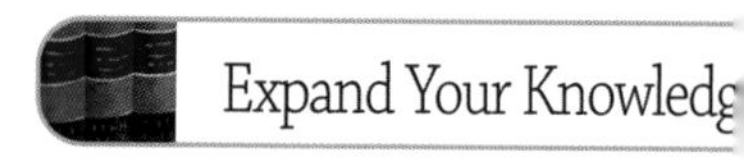

Principle #11

Belief that Hashem rewards those who obey the commandments of the Torah and punishes those who violate its prohibitions

אֲנִי מַאֲמִין בֶּאֱמוּנָה שְׁלֵמָה, שֶׁהַבּוֹרֵא יִתְבָּרַךְ שְׁמוֹ גּוֹמֵל טוֹב לְשׁוֹמְרֵי מִצְוֹתָיו וּמַעֲנִישׁ לְעוֹבְרֵי מִצְוֹתָיו.

I believe with complete faith that the Creator, Blessed is His Name, rewards those who obey His commandments and punishes those who violate His commandments.

גּוֹמֵל לְאִישׁ חֶסֶד כְּמִפְעָלוֹ, נוֹתֵן לְרָשָׁע רָע כְּרִשְׁעָתוֹ.

Principle #12

Belief that Mashiach will come

אֲנִי מַאֲמִין בֶּאֱמוּנָה שְׁלֵמָה בְּבִיאַת הַמָּשִׁיחַ, וְאַף עַל פִּי שֶׁיִּתְמַהְמֵהַּ, עִם כָּל זֶה אֲחַכֶּה לּוֹ בְּכָל יוֹם שֶׁיָּבוֹא.

I believe with complete faith in the coming of Mashiach, and even though he may delay, even so, I will wait every day for him to come.

יִשְׁלַח לְקֵץ הַיָּמִין מְשִׁיחֵנוּ, לִפְדּוֹת מְחַכֵּי קֵץ יְשׁוּעָתוֹ.

Principle #13

Belief that Hashem will bring the dead back to life

אֲנִי מַאֲמִין בֶּאֱמוּנָה שְׁלֵמָה, שֶׁתִּהְיֶה תְּחִיַּת הַמֵּתִים בְּעֵת שֶׁיַּעֲלֶה רָצוֹן מֵאֵת הַבּוֹרֵא, יִתְבָּרַךְ שְׁמוֹ, וְיִתְעַלֶּה זִכְרוֹ לָעַד וּלְנֵצַח נְצָחִים.

I believe with complete faith that the dead will be brought to life at the time when Hashem, Blessed is His Name, wishes it to happen, and His Name will be exalted forever and for all eternity.

מֵתִים יְחַיֶּה קֵל בְּרֹב חַסְדּוֹ, בָּרוּךְ עֲדֵי עַד שֵׁם תְּהִלָּתוֹ.

Determine Mastery

REVIEWING KEY INFORMATION

1. How would you define emunah in Hashem?
2. Why did Avraham seek out Noach and Shem?
3. How is emunah the foundation of all the מצוות?
4. Both Avraham and Unkelos came to understand that Hashem is the Creator. How did each one come to this conclusion?

CRITICAL THINKING

1. How does the unbroken chain from Avraham enable our emunah to remain strong?
2. What are the שֵׁשׁ מִצְווֹת תְּמִידִיּוֹת, and how can we fulfill them in our daily lives?

INVESTIGATE AND INQUIRE

1. The Gemara (מכות 23b-24a) states: Six hundred and thirteen מצוות were given to Yisrael ... Chavakuk came (see Chavakuk 2:4) and summed them all up in just one: וְצַדִּיק בֶּאֱמוּנָתוֹ יִחְיֶה, And the righteous person lives by his faith. Based on your understanding of the mitzvah of emunah, what do you think the Gemara is teaching us?

In loving memory of
our dear father
ר' יהודה לייב בן ר' ישראל ז"ל

James and Elana Fendelman
St. Louis, Missouri

מצוה

כו

MITZVAH 26

Do Not Believe in Other gods

איסור האמונה באלהים אחרים

MITZVAH 26

איסור האמונה באלהים אחרים

Do Not Believe in Other gods

THE MITZVAH

It is forbidden to believe that any god other than Hashem exists.

- אִסוּר
- מוֹשֵׁל
- שַׁלִּיט
- שׁוֹפֵט
- לַאו
- לַאו שֶׁאֵין בּוֹ מַעֲשֶׂה
- כּוֹפֵר בְּעִקָּר
- טֶבַע
- מִלְּבַדּוֹ
- נְבִיאֵי שֶׁקֶר

SECTION I Introduction to the Mitzvah

In this world, a leader cannot do his job alone. A president, for example, has a cabinet; a king has his advisers. These people not only assist the ruler in making decisions, but the ruler grants them certain power to make decisions without consulting him. Hashem, however, has limitless power and has no need for assistants or advisers. Any power He gives to any of His creations is dependent upon His will. The sun gives us daylight and heat only because Hashem gives it the ability to do so.

Throughout history, there were people who believed in Hashem, but they also believed that Hashem gave His creations powers as well. They believed that Hashem shared His powers with things like the sun and the stars, and wanted people to worship them.

This mitzvah is teaching us that it is not enough to believe that Hashem exists. We must also know that Hashem is the only God and there is no other. Nothing else has any power. There is no creator (בּוֹרֵא) but Hashem. Hashem is the only One Who can create something from nothing (יֵשׁ מֵאַיִן). Everything is made by His Hand, and nothing exists in this world by chance. He is the Ruler (מוֹשֵׁל) over the entire universe, He controls everything (שַׁלִּיט), and His mastery is solitary and absolute. He guides (מַשְׁגִּיחַ) all His creations individually. He is the Judge (שׁוֹפֵט) of all the earth and all that is in it, and directs everything that happens.

~ see דעת תבונות §36

When we believe that Hashem is the only God, the One God, and that there is no other, then our belief in Hashem is complete and the foundation of our faith is secure.

In what way does the mitzvah of לֹא יִהְיֶה לְךָ complete Mitzvah 25, אָנֹכִי ה׳?

The Source of the Mitzvah

SECTION II

לֹא יִהְיֶה לְךָ אֱלֹהִים אֲחֵרִים עַל פָּנָי

שמות כ:ג פרשת יתרו

Do not recognize other gods before Me

According to the Rambam, a person violates this prohibition simply by believing in his mind that there are other gods besides Hashem. He does not have to perform an act or even express his thoughts in order to violate this prohibition.

That is why, some Acharonim explain, the פסוק says "לֹא יִהְיֶה "לְךָ. The word לך means *for you*; do not have a belief in other gods in the privacy of your mind, a sin which is *for you,* known only to you and not to anyone else but Hashem.

~ see *Biurei Maharshal* to *Smag,* לא תעשה §1

Reading Check

What does the word לך in the פסוק come to teach us?

Did You Know?

Because the aveirah of believing in other gods is so terrible, Chazal prohibited the repeating of certain expressions during prayer, as they can be interpreted as being addressed to two separate gods. For example, a person may not repeat the phrase מוֹדִים אֲנַחְנוּ לָךְ (We thank You) twice in a row during the Shemoneh Esrei, even if he means to refer only to Hashem.

~ ברכות 33b; *Rambam,* הלכות תפילה 9:4

It is forbidden to believe that any god other than Hashem exists.

SECTION III The Laws of the Mitzvah

1. A person violates this prohibition simply by believing that another god exists. If he acts on his belief and actively serves his "god," then he violates Mitzvah 28 — *Do Not Bow Down to an* עבודה זרה, Mitzvah 29 — *Do Not Worship an* עבודה זרה, or both, depending upon how he worships it.

2. In order for a person to violate this prohibition, he must believe that his "god" has the free will and power to make its own choices, and the ability to act upon those choices.

3. A person violates this prohibition even if he believes that Hashem is the ultimate Power, and gave another "god" some powers.

4. This mitzvah is one of the six constant מצוות (שֵׁשׁ מִצְוֹות תְּמִידִיּוֹת). A person is obligated in these six מצוות every moment of his entire life, and is rewarded each moment that he thinks about them.

5. This mitzvah applies to both men and women, in all places and at all times. As a general rule, all of the Torah's prohibitions (מצוות לא תעשה) apply equally to men and women.

6. A person who believes that another god exists other than Hashem rejects the fundamental principle of Judaism (he is a כּוֹפֵר בָּעִקָּר). This person, however, is not punished by בית דין, since he has violated a לַאו שֶׁאֵין בּוֹ מַעֲשֶׂה, *a prohibition that involves no action*. Generally, בית דין will only punish a person for an action, not a thought. However, if the person puts his belief into practice and serves his "god," then he is liable to punishment from בית דין.

טוב טעם
Appreciating the Mitzvah

Mitzvah 25 and Mitzvah 26 Go Hand in Hand

When a person fulfills this mitzvah and does not believe in any "god" other than Hashem, it completes his *emunah* in Hashem. A person does not truly believe in Hashem if he believes that there are other "gods" or powers other than Hashem. This is why, say Chazal, the first and second commandments were said by Hashem at the same time; because they are dependent upon one another. The fulfillment of one is impossible without the other.

~ *Yalkut Shimoni, Yirmiah* §266, עקידת יצחק §45

Just as our acceptance of the Torah and מצוות depends upon our belief in Hashem (Mitzvah 25), so, too, it depends upon our fulfillment of this mitzvah. Only a person who believes with complete faith in Hashem as the only God can truly accept the עוֹל הַמִּצְווֹת.

~ *Biur Maharan Zak* to *Smag*, לא תעשה §1

Trust in Hashem Alone

Hashem has many Names, and each one describes a different aspect of His מידות. When the Name "אלקים" is used, it describes Hashem as the "Master over all powers." If a person places his hope in any phenomenon (such as nature), thinking it will help him find sustenance, livelihood, or healing, then, in a sense, he is guilty of believing in אלהים אחרים, *other gods,* for he is attributing power to something other than Hashem, Who is the Master over all powers.

טֶבַע, *nature,* itself was created by Hashem, and although a person must live by the laws of nature, he should not place his trust in them. He should rather place his trust in ה' אלקים, the Master of all power, Who controls all natural causes according to His will.

~ *Derech Pikudecha*, לא תעשה §26-29, *Cheilek HaMachshavah* §7

This concept, explains the Abarbanel, is hinted in the fact that the פסוק of אָנֹכִי ה' אֱלֹקֶיךָ אֲשֶׁר הוֹצֵאתִיךָ מֵאֶרֶץ מִצְרַיִם is immediately followed by לֹא יִהְיֶה לְךָ אֱלֹהִים אֲחֵרִים עַל פָּנָי. After

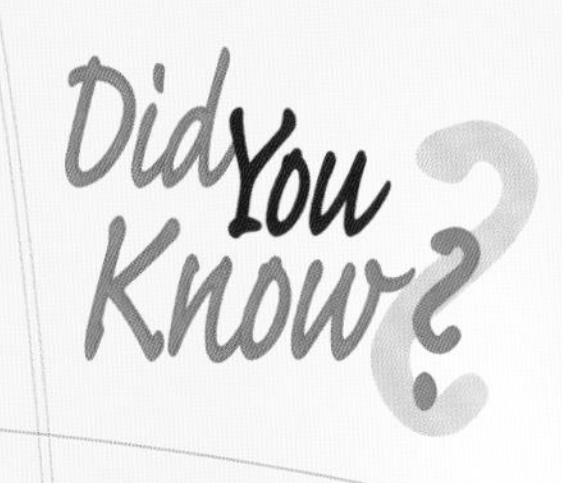

When Rosh Hashanah arrives, the מלאכים say to Hashem, "Master of the universe, why do You show Bnei Yisrael so much kindness, as a man would show his best friend?" Hashem answers them and says, "It is because of the devotion of Avraham, their father. When Terach, Avraham's father, asked him to sell his idols in the market-place, Avraham smashed them, and sanctified My Name."

~ see *Tanna D'Vei Eliyahu* 25:5

It is forbidden to believe that any god other than Hashem exists.

Hashem demonstrated, through the miraculous way He took us out of Mitzrayim, His complete control over the laws of nature, how can we turn away from Him and place our trust in natural forces?

~ *Abarbanel*, שמות 20:3

אין עוד מלבדו

The פסוק (דברים 4:35) states: אַתָּה הָרְאֵתָ לָדַעַת, כִּי ה׳ הוּא הָאֱלֹקִים, אֵין עוֹד מִלְּבַדּוֹ, *You have been shown to know that Hashem, He is the God; there is none besides Him!* Rashi comments on this פסוק that at the time of מתן תורה, Hashem opened up the seven heavens to show Bnei Yisrael that He is the only Master of the upper and lower worlds. Bnei Yisrael were clearly shown that there is none besides Hashem.

The concept of אֵין עוֹד מִלְּבַדּוֹ means that not only is there no other god besides Hashem, but that there is no power anywhere that can do anything without His decree, for Hashem is the Master over all powers.

Similarly, if a person is smart or talented in some way, he should not place his trust in his abilities. He must always remain aware that Hashem is the One Who gives him his talents, and his success is always in Hashem's hands.

~ see צדקת הצדיק §232

R' Chaim Volozhin, the famous talmid of the Vilna Gaon, tells us that if a person feels threatened by some sort of danger, he should concentrate all his thoughts on the concept that Hashem is the only true Source of power, and that there is no other besides Him (אֵין עוֹד מִלְּבַדּוֹ). If he wholeheartedly believes that nothing can happen to him unless Hashem decrees it so, then the threat will not harm him.

~ *Nefesh HaChaim* 3:12

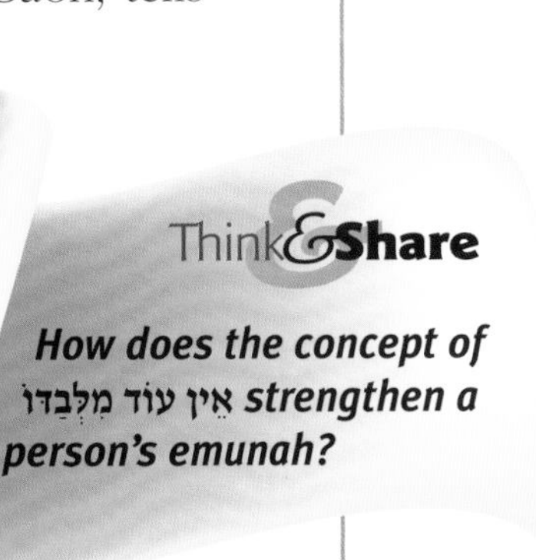

Think&Share

How does the concept of אֵין עוֹד מִלְּבַדּוֹ strengthen a person's emunah?

MITZVAH 25
MITZVAH 26
MITZVAH 27
MITZVAH 28
MITZVAH 29
MITZVAH 30
MITZVAH 31
MITZVAH 32
MITZVAH 33
MITZVAH 34
MITZVAH 35
MITZVAH 36
MITZVAH 37
MITZVAH 38

Living the Mitzvah

How עבודה זרה Began

From the time of Enosh, through the time of Avraham Avinu, to Eliyahu HaNavi at Har HaCarmel, and until the destruction of בית ראשון*, the temptation of* עבודה זרה *was a constant struggle for the Jewish people and the other nations of the world. This terrible sin was one of the causes of the destruction of the first* בית המקדש*. Our* חכמים *foresaw that the generations to come would not be able to withstand the temptation of* עבודה זרה*, so they prayed for Hashem to remove it from Bnei Yisrael. But how did* עבודה זרה *even begin? When did the people start forgetting that Hashem is the only God?*

It was in the time of Enosh, the son of שֵׁת and the grandson of אדם הראשון. The descendants of אדם were multiplying and covering the land. The people worked hard at earning their livelihood. Some were farmers, and some were shepherds. Their day-to-day existence

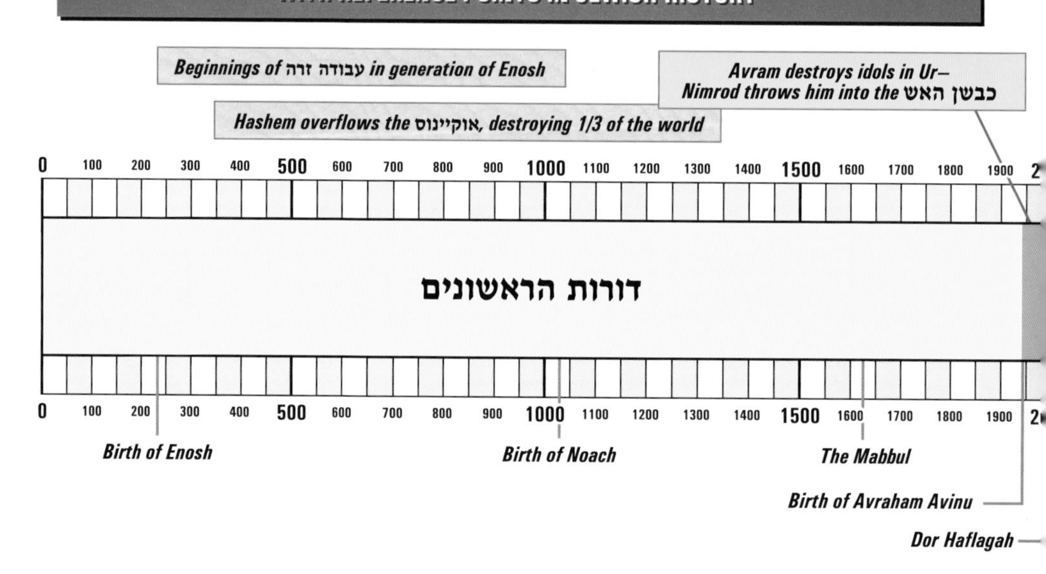

It is forbidden to believe that any god other than Hashem exists.

was not easy. Of course, they knew why they had to live this kind of life; why they were not in גן עדן. They knew that Hashem Himself had fashioned אדם into the first man, out of the earth, and that אדם had walked the paths of גן עדן! He had lived on the highest spiritual level man can achieve, only to sin and fall. אדם had been so close to Hashem! Even שֵׁת, who was born after his parents were expelled from גן עדן, was still on a very high spiritual level. But the generations were multiplying, and they were moving further and further away from those exalted men. "How can we," the people thought, "possibly pray directly to Hashem? We are not worthy like our fathers!"

The people looked at the sun, the moon, and the stars and they said, "Hashem created the sun, moon, and stars and put them in the sky to govern the world's days and nights. Surely if Hashem has accorded them such honor, He would want us to accord them honor as well!" So they began to worship the sun, the moon, and the stars.

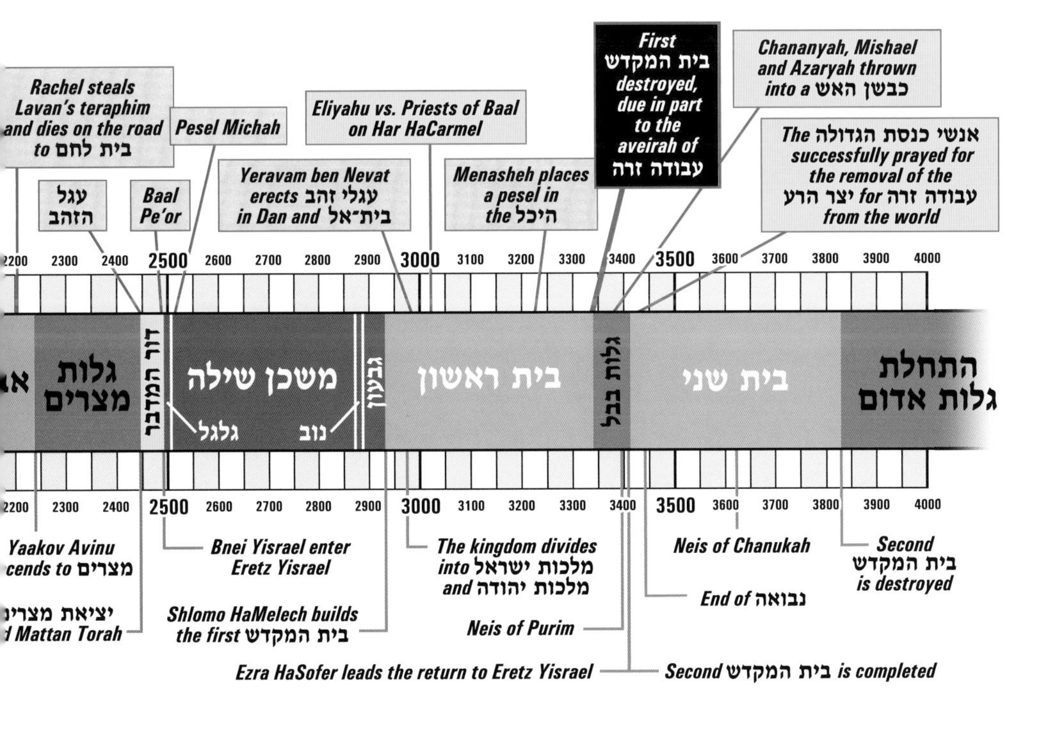

The sculptures depicted do not represent actual idols that were worshipped. They are included merely to present the reader with an understanding of the events which took place in the story.

The people liked this way of worship, and started to build altars and put up beautiful structures to honor and serve these representatives.

As time passed, false prophets arose and claimed that Hashem had appeared to them, and wanted the people to worship the stars, or a specific star. The people followed these נְבִיאֵי שֶׁקֶר and began to worship these stars, and to build statues and idols of them. Other deceivers then came forward, claiming that they had been spoken to by the stars themselves, and that they had been told how the star wished to be worshipped. The people eventually forgot why they had started worshipping the sun, the moon, and the stars. They began worshipping them, no longer as emissaries of Hashem, no longer because they thought Hashem wanted them to revere the celestial bodies, but as gods themselves, who had the power to help or harm them. They carved sculptures and idols of the heavenly images using metals, wood, and

It is forbidden to believe that any god other than Hashem exists.

stone, built altars to them and offered sacrifices to the idols themselves. The majority of mankind soon forgot Hashem completely. Only a few individuals remained who believed in the One Hashem.

The people's actions angered Hashem, Who decided to punish them severely. He wanted them to recognize once more that Hashem is the only God. Hashem caused the waters of the אוקיינוס to overflow and destroy many of the idol worshippers. Chazal tell us that this disaster destroyed one-third of the world.

But the people did not learn their lesson and do תְּשׁוּבָה. Even though so many of them had been killed, they continued to sin against Hashem.

Though at certain times, the people served only Hashem, Bnei Yisrael continued to worship עבודה זרה throughout history. Until the destruction of בית ראשון, the temptation to serve idols remained irresistibly strong. The יצר הרע for עבודה זרה was so strong that the חכמים prayed to Hashem to remove it from the hearts of Bnei Yisrael, and Hashem did as they asked. (See Mitzvah 29 Section V.)

However, there was a price to be paid for the removal of the יצר הרע for עבודה זרה. When Bnei Yisrael succumbed to the temptation to worship עבודה זרה, they distanced themselves from the שכינה. However, when they turned their backs on עבודה זרה and did not listen to the very persuasive יצר הרע, then they would draw closer to Hashem. This earned them the privilege of נבואה, for prophecy is direct communication between man and Hashem.

When the אַנְשֵׁי כְּנֶסֶת הַגְּדוֹלָה succeeded in removing the יצר הרע for עבודה זרה, Bnei Yisrael lost the privilege of having נבואה. But the אַנְשֵׁי כְּנֶסֶת הַגְּדוֹלָה, having seen the destructive influence of the יצר הרע for עבודה זרה, knew that the price of losing נבואה was worth paying to ensure the survival of our nation.

So devastating was the evil inclination for עבודה זרה that the חכמים accepted this exchange for the benefit of Bnei Yisrael.

FOCUS

Why did people start worshipping עבודה זרה?

Expand Your Knowledge

SECTION VI

Praying at the Gravesite of a Tzaddik

It is customary to pray at the grave of a deceased *tzaddik*. This is permitted, and is not a violation of the לַאו of לֹא יִהְיֶה לְךָ אֱלֹהִים אֲחֵרִים, as long as we are praying to Hashem and not to the deceased.

It is customary to pray at the gravesite of a *tzaddik* for one of the following reasons:

a. The gravesite of a *tzaddik* is a holy place, and our prayers will be accepted more readily in such a place.

~ *Maharil*, הלכות ראש השנה §63; *Mishnah Berurah* 581:27

b. The merit of the *tzaddik* lends support to one who prays at his gravesite.

~ see *Levush*, end of §579

c. There is a flow of Heavenly blessing that comes to the world because of a *tzaddik*, even after his death, and we hope that our prayers at his gravesite will connect us with that flow.

~ דרשת הר"ן §8

We find in the Torah an instance where a person prayed at the gravesite of *tzaddikim*. The Torah states (במדבר 13:22) that when the *Meraglim* (the spies sent to scout out Eretz Yisrael) entered the land, "he" came to Chevron. The Gemara (*Sotah* 34b) explains that only one of the spies, Calev ben Yefuneh, went to Chevron, to pray at the מְעָרַת הַמַּכְפֵּלָה, the gravesite of the אבות. He prayed to Hashem that he should be saved from the evil plan of the *Meraglim*, and Hashem granted his request.

Determine Mastery

REVIEWING KEY INFORMATION

1. In order to make our emunah complete, what else do we have to believe about Hashem aside from the fact that He exists and that He is the only God?
2. How can a person violate this prohibition without performing an action?
3. Why won't בית דין punish someone for believing there are other gods (if he does not actually worship them)?
4. Why do we use the term אלהים אחרים to refer to עבודה זרה?

CRITICAL THINKING

1. After learning this mitzvah, what do you think is an accurate description of "nature"?

לכבוד הורי היקרים

ר' לוי ומרת חיינע בת-שבע מאלגי שיחיו

שיזכו לראות רוב נחת

מתוך בריאות הגוף ואושר וכבוד

מצאצאיהם עד סוף כל הדורות

מצוה

27

MITZVAH

Do Not Make an Idol or an Image

איסור עשיית פסל

MITZVAH **27**

איסור עשיית פסל

Do Not Make an Idol or an Image

THE MITZVAH

A person is forbidden to make or hire someone else to make idols (such as sculptures) or images (such as pictures, portraits, or engravings) for his own worship.

- לֵצִים
- מַסֵּכָה
- הֲנָאָה
- מִדְּאוֹרַיְתָא
- מִדְּרַבָּנָן
- מַלְקוּת
- יֵהָרֵג וְאַל יַעֲבֹר
- סְיָג
- עוֹלֶה רֶגֶל

MITZVAH 25 | MITZVAH 26 | MITZVAH 27 | MITZVAH 28 | MITZVAH 29 | MITZVAH 30 | MITZVAH 31 | MITZVAH 32 | MITZVAH 33 | MITZVAH 34 | MITZVAH 35 | MITZVAH 36 | MITZVAH 37 | MITZVAH 38

SECTION I

Introduction to the Mitzvah

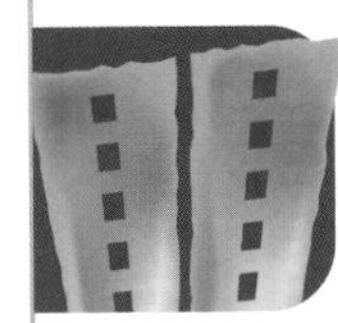

The police put the two men in handcuffs, escorted them out of the building, and padlocked the door so that no one could enter. The men were soon brought to trial for their crime — operating a bomb factory.

The judge gave them the maximum sentence. Startled and dismayed, the defendants could not believe their ears. "We only made the bombs," they exclaimed. "We never used them! We didn't hurt anyone!"

The judge told them, "We are indeed fortunate that you did not get a chance to use the bombs you manufactured. But once you were making them, what else were you going to do with them but use them?"

The road to עבודה זרה is no different. If we want to avoid עבודה זרה, we must not even take that first step.

דוד המלך wrote in *Sefer Tehillim* (1:1), אַשְׁרֵי הָאִישׁ אֲשֶׁר לֹא הָלַךְ בַּעֲצַת רְשָׁעִים וּבְדֶרֶךְ חַטָּאִים לֹא עָמָד וּבְמוֹשַׁב לֵצִים לֹא יָשָׁב, *Fortunate is the man who has not walked in the counsel of the wicked, who has not stood in the pathway of the sinful, and has not sat in a session of scoffers.* The Gemara (עבודה זרה 18b) asks: If a man did not even walk in the counsel of the wicked, then surely he could not have stood in their path. And if he never stood in their path, he most certainly never sat with them! What is the meaning of these words of דוד המלך?

The Gemara explains: דוד המלך is telling us that if one merely walks in the counsel of the wicked, meaning upon a sinful path, he will find himself standing near sin, even if he tells himself that he will just watch. And once he has stood upon such a path, he will eventually sit, joining the company of לֵצִים, *mockers.* And if he sits with them, before long he himself will take part in their mockery.

With this prohibition, the Torah is teaching us that if we want to avoid עבודה זרה, we must not even walk in its path. Someone who creates an idol has taken the first step toward worshipping עבודה זרה. For this reason the Torah forbids even *making* an idol. For if a person makes an עבודה זרה, he will eventually come to bow down to it. And once he has bowed down to it, he will certainly come to serve it.

~ *Rabbeinu Bachya,* שמות 20:4; *Chinuch* §27

Think&Share

What is the first idol mentioned in the Torah?

The Source of the Mitzvah

SECTION II

לֹא תַעֲשֶׂה לְךָ פֶסֶל וְכָל תְּמוּנָה

שמות כ:ד פרשת יתרו

Do not make for yourself an idol or any image

A similar mitzvah (Mitzvah 214) appears in פרשת קדושים. There (ויקרא 19:4) the Torah states: וֵאלֹהֵי מַסֵּכָה לֹא תַעֲשׂוּ לָכֶם, *And molten gods* (idols made from molten metal) *you shall not make for yourselves.*

There are two basic differences between these two מצוות:

1. This mitzvah, Mitzvah 27, prohibits a person to make an idol himself, or to hire a person to make the idol for him. Mitzvah 214 only prohibits a person to make idols, but not to hire someone to do it for him.
2. This mitzvah prohibits a person to make an idol for his own use, while Mitzvah 214 prohibits a person to make an idol even for others to use.

~ *Rambam,* ספר המצוות, לא תעשה §3

Did You Know?

Chazal explain לא תעשה לך פסל as also teaching: Do not make "of" yourself an idol. A person is not allowed to try to convince others to worship him.

~ *Sanhedrin* 61a

Similarly, Yaakov Avinu did not want to be buried in Mitzrayim, because he did not want the Egyptians to worship him as an עבודה זרה.

~ בראשית רבה 96:5

What are the differences between Mitzvah 27 and Mitzvah 214?

A person is forbidden to make or hire someone else to make idols (such as sculptures) or images (such as pictures, portraits, or engravings) for his own worship.

SECTION III The Laws of the Mitzvah

1. This prohibition forbids a person to make any idol or image for the purpose of worshipping it. The prohibition against the actual worship of idols is the subject of Mitzvah 28 and Mitzvah 29.

2. A person violates this prohibition either by making idols or images himself, or by hiring others to make them for him.

3. This prohibition is violated when the idol or image is completed, even if, in the end, it is not worshipped.

4. A person cannot derive any benefit (הֲנָאָה) from idols or anything used in idol worship. However, by Torah law (מִדְּאוֹרַיְתָא), a person who is hired to make an idol may use the money he has been paid (even though he has committed a terrible sin). However, some Rishonim rule that the money is forbidden Rabbinically (מִדְּרַבָּנָן).

5. One who violates this prohibition in the presence of valid witnesses, after having been warned (הַתְרָאָה), receives מַלְקוּת, *lashes*.

6. One must sacrifice his life rather than worship idols. This is one of the three מצוות that a Jew must not violate, even if it means giving up his life (יֵהָרֵג וְאַל יַעֲבֹר). Some authorities say that a person must sacrifice his life rather than commit any sin connected to these three sins. According to this opinion, a person must sacrifice his life rather than make an idol.

7. This prohibition applies to both men and women, in all places and at all times. As a general rule, all of the Torah's prohibitions (מצוות לא תעשה) apply equally to men and women. Non-Jews are prohibited from making idols as well, because this is included in the prohibition against idolatry, which is one of the שֶׁבַע מִצְוֹות בְּנֵי נֹחַ.

Note: One who makes an idol or image for someone else violates Mitzvah 214. For the positive mitzvah to destroy idols and images, see Mitzvah 436.

MITZVAH 25 MITZVAH 26 MITZVAH 27 MITZVAH 28 MITZVAH 29 MITZVAH 30 MITZVAH 31 MITZVAH 32 MITZVAH 33 MITZVAH 34 MITZVAH 35 MITZVAH 36 MITZVAH 37 MITZVAH 38

טוב טעם
Appreciating the Mitzvah

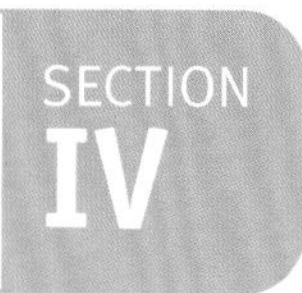

Can You Make an Image of Hashem?

The Torah prohibits not only the creation of an image or idol representing עבודה זרה or natural forces — it also prohibits creating an idol or image that is meant to represent Hashem Himself.

One of the Rambam's Thirteen Principles of Faith states: I believe with complete faith that the Creator, Blessed is His Name, has no physical body and physical concepts do not apply to Him, and there is nothing that can compare to Him at all.

To make a form or image so that one can become more "aware" of Hashem's Presence is dangerous and wrong. It gives the impression that there is something to which we can compare Hashem, and this is absolutely false. Hashem cannot be seen, and His Essence is beyond human comprehension. As the Navi Yeshayah says (40:18): וְאֶל מִי תְּדַמְּיוּן קֵל וּמַה דְּמוּת תַּעַרְכוּ לוֹ, *To whom do you compare God, and what form can you create for Him?*

~ *R.Y. Bechor Shor,* שמות 20:4

Gods of Gold and Silver

Actual idols or images are not the only kind of עבודה זרה a person is forbidden to make. A person is forbidden to make a "god" out of anything. In פרשת יתרו, the Torah specifically forbids the making of gods out of silver and gold, as the פסוק states (שמות 20:20): אֱלֹהֵי כֶסֶף וֵאלֹהֵי זָהָב לֹא תַעֲשׂוּ לָכֶם, *gods of silver and gods of gold you shall not make for yourselves.* When a person is driven by the desire for material wealth until that pursuit takes up all of his time and energy, then he is guilty of making money into an "idol." His worship of this "idol" becomes his focus, and it replaces Hashem and the Torah in his life.

~ עקידת יצחק §45

One who does find himself in a position of wealth must be extra careful to always keep the Torah and מצוות as the focal point of his life. He must always remember that all his wealth comes from Hashem, and never think (דברים 8:17): כֹּחִי וְעֹצֶם יָדִי עָשָׂה לִי אֶת

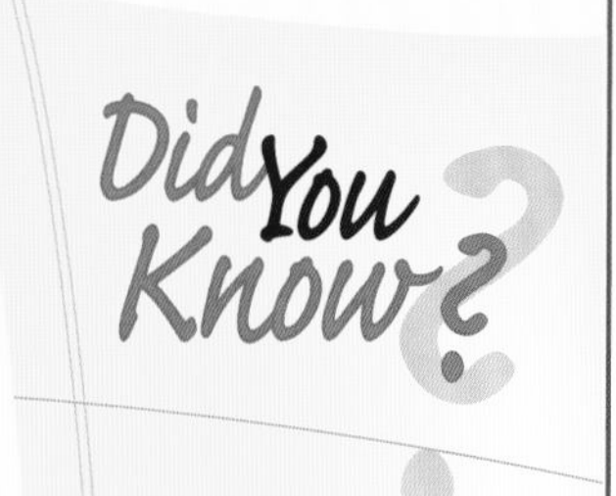

Chur, the son of Miriam, was murdered when he tried to stop Bnei Yisrael from making the עגל הזהב. Because he tried to stop Bnei Yisrael from creating an idol, his grandson, Betzalel, merited to build the Mishkan, where the שכינה dwelled, and all its כלים as well.

~ שמות רבה 48:3

MITZVAH 27

A person is forbidden to make or hire someone else to make idols (such as sculptures) or images (such as pictures, portraits, or engravings) for his own worship.

MITZVAH 25
MITZVAH 26
MITZVAH 27
MITZVAH 28
MITZVAH 29
MITZVAH 30
MITZVAH 31
MITZVAH 32
MITZVAH 33
MITZVAH 34
MITZVAH 35
MITZVAH 36
MITZVAH 37
MITZVAH 38

הַחַיִל הַזֶּה, *My strength and the might of my hand made me all this wealth*. This is a נִסָּיוֹן that Hashem gives to those He feels can use their wealth and prosperity to accomplish good deeds.

~ see דרשות רבינו יונה, שמות 20:20

עשו סיג לתורה

The Mishnah (אבות 1:1) urges us: עֲשׂוּ סְיָג לַתּוֹרָה, *Make a fence around the Torah,* so you will not even come close to performing an *aveirah*. When it comes to עבודה זרה, the Torah itself made that fence for us, by telling us not to even make an idol.

There are over a dozen פסוקים in the Torah that deal with the prohibition against making idols and images. They include prohibitions against making representations of angels, living creatures, heavenly bodies, and anything found on earth.

The *Mechilta* explains that the Torah goes to such great lengths to list all these examples so that we will never come to make a mistake and worship one of these things. The desire to worship idols was so strong that Hashem did not want the יצר הרע to be able to point at an object and say to a person, "That's not a god — that's the sun! The Torah does not prohibit making an image of this." Therefore, Hashem made sure that the Torah was very explicit and listed everything that a person might worship other than Hashem. In this way, there are no loopholes for the יצר הרע to seize upon and use against us.

~ see *Mechilta* to שמות 20:4

Hashem gave us this prohibition to keep us far away from sin. Chazal, too, gave us many גְּזֵרוֹת דְּרַבָּנָן, *Rabbinic decrees*. Chazal, in their wisdom and foresight, enacted these laws so that we will not come to do עבירות that the Torah prohibits. Included in these laws are many of our הלכות שבת, such as *muktzah*.

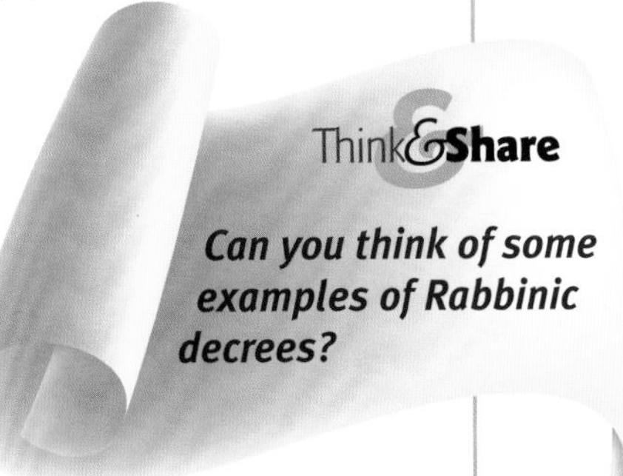

Living the Mitzvah

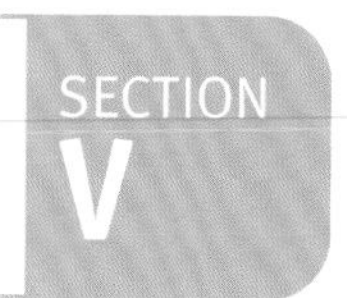

SECTION V

The Golden Calves of Yeravam ben Nevat

Until the death of Shlomo HaMelech, there was only one kingdom in Eretz Yisrael — מלכות בית דוד. However, toward the end of Shlomo HaMelech's life, some of his wives turned his heart away from Hashem, and he did not prevent them from worshipping עבודה זרה. Therefore, Hashem decreed that, after Shlomo's death, his kingdom would be divided.

The two kingdoms during the reign of Yeravam ben Nevat.

⦿ Cities where Yeravam erected golden calves and a temple area
★ Capital city ▲ Mountain peak

Hashem sent the Navi, Achiyah HaShiloni, to tell Yeravam ben Nevat that he had been chosen to be the king over the new kingdom. Hashem promised Yeravam that if he followed in Hashem's ways, Hashem would be with him, and would build a dynasty from his house just as He had done with the house of דוד.

The tribes of Binyamin and Yehudah remained loyal to Rechavam, Shlomo's son and heir. However, the other ten tribes separated from the kingdom of Yehudah, and created מלכות ישראל. They appointed Yeravam ben Nevat as their king.

Yeravam was no ordinary man. He was a great תלמיד חכם. He could have been a great *tzaddik* and led his people to lofty spiritual heights. But Yeravam became haughty, and his desire for honor led not only him, but the people in his kingdom as well, down the terrible path of עבודה זרה.

"The first time all the people go up to Yerushalayim to be עוֹלֶה רֶגֶל on the festival," he

A person is forbidden to make or hire someone else to make idols (such as sculptures) or images (such as pictures, portraits, or engravings) for his own worship.

thought, "they will not come back. They will no longer accept me as king, for no one may sit in the courtyard of the בית המקדש except the king descended from the house of דוד המלך. If Rechavam sits, and I do not, the people will think, 'Rechavam is the true king. Yeravam is not a king at all!' And if I dare sit, the people will think that I am rebelling against the monarchy of Yehudah, and I will be put to death. My only hope is to stop the people from going up to Yerushalayim!"

Yeravam decided to build altars, complete with idols, in his own kingdom, and to tell the people to travel there instead of going to Yerushalayim. But first he needed to make sure that the righteous men that made up a portion of his advisers would not turn against him when he suggested that the people should worship idols. To accomplish this, he came up with a devious plan. He convened all of his advisers, and sat them so the wicked ones and righteous ones were intermingled, with a wicked adviser sitting next to each righteous one. He then asked them all, "Will you sign a document that you support all of my actions?"

"Yes!" came the answer.

"Do you accept me as king?"

"Yes!" they all replied.

"Will you listen to my decrees?"

"Yes!" they said once more.

"Even if I decree that the people should serve idols?" asked Yeravam.

The righteous men cried out, "Heaven forbid!" An evil adviser turned to a righteous one and asked him, "Do you really think such a man as Yeravam would serve idols? He is just testing us, to see if we trust his judgment."

All the wicked men then rose and signed the document. The righteous advisers, fooled by this trickery, signed the document as well. Thus, the whole council signed the document approving all of

The sculptures depicted do not represent actual idols that were worshipped. They are included merely to present the reader with an understanding of the events which took place in the story.

Yeravam's actions. Now, Yeravam had the power to do as he pleased, and no one could stop him in protest, for even the righteous ones had signed the document.

Yeravam then fashioned two golden calves. He placed one in בית-אל and one in Dan. And he proclaimed to his subjects, "It is too far for you to go up to Yerushalayim. These are your gods, O Yisrael, who brought you up from the land of Mitzrayim!" He declared his own holiday on the fifteenth of Cheshvan. He appointed his own priests who were not Kohanim. He closed all the borders, posting guards so the people could not go up to Yerushalayim, under penalty of death.

Yeravam ben Nevat is a prime example of one who sinned and caused others to sin as well. Until the sin of Yeravam ben Nevat, Bnei Yisrael were only suffering from the effects of one golden calf, the עגל

A person is forbidden to make or hire someone else to make idols (such as sculptures) or images (such as pictures, portraits, or engravings) for his own worship.

הזהב they had made in the *Midbar*. Now, their sins had multiplied, and they suffered from the effects of two additional golden calves, the calves of Yeravam ben Nevat.

Even though Yeravam's sin was great, Hashem still would have accepted his תשובה. Hashem "grabbed" Yeravam by his cloak and said to him, "Repent! Then I, you, and the son of Yishai (דוד המלך) will stroll together in Gan Eden."

Yeravam asked Hashem, "Who will go first? I or the son of Yishai?"

Hashem answered, "The son of Yishai will lead."

Yeravam replied, "Then I am not interested." Yeravam never repented, and has no share in עולם הבא.

Because Yeravam sinned and caused others to sin, and because he would not repent, Hashem decreed a horrible punishment for him and his entire house. As it states in *Melachim* I (14:7-11): So said Hashem, God of Yisrael, "I elevated you from the midst of the people and placed you as ruler over My people, Yisrael, and I tore the kingship away from the House of דוד and gave it to you. But you were never like דוד, who kept My commandments and who followed Me with all his heart, doing only what was upright in My eyes. And you have acted more wickedly that any who came before you, for you went and made for yourself other "gods" and molten images to anger Me, and you have thrown Me behind your back. Therefore, behold! I am bringing evil upon the house of Yeravam, and I shall cut down every male offspring of Yeravam... Anyone of the house of Yeravam who dies in the city, will be eaten by the dogs; and whoever dies in the field, will be eaten by the birds."

FOCUS

How did Yeravam deceive his righteous advisers into signing a decree that allowed idol worship into מלכות ישראל?

Of course, Hashem's words came to pass. Yeravam's family was killed by Baasha, the son of Achiyah (not the Navi). He killed Nadav, Yeravam's son, who ascended the throne after the death of his father. Baasha then became king, and killed out Yeravam's entire household.

Expand Your Knowledge

SECTION VI

Question: The punishment for violating this prohibition is מַלְקוּת, *lashes*. We can easily understand why a person receives this punishment if he himself makes the idol or image. However, a person violates this prohibition even if he hires someone else to make the idol. Usually, one does not receive מַלְקוּת for a לַאו שֶׁאֵין בּוֹ מַעֲשֶׂה, violating a מצות לא תעשה that does not involve a physical action. Hiring someone to do a job (even a sinful job) is not an action. Why, then, does a person who hired another to create an idol receive מַלְקוּת?

The Acharonim offer several answers to this question:

1 In this case, the person's words (when he hired the worker) resulted in a forbidden action, and therefore the words themselves are considered an action.

~ מנחת חינוך 27:1

2 The person receives מַלְקוּת not for hiring the person to make the idol, but for taking possession of it after it is made.

~ *S'dei Chemed*, vol. 4 מערכת ל' §12

3 Although generally, a person does not receive מַלְקוּת for a לַאו שֶׁאֵין בּוֹ מַעֲשֶׂה, the Torah made an exception when it came to the very serious *aveirah* of עבודה זרה.

~ *S'dei Chemed*, ibid.

According to the Sefer HaChinuch, a person who hires another person to make an idol has *not* violated this prohibition; rather, the *maker* of the idol violates the prohibition. This is because the Sefer HaChinuch holds that a person who makes idols for others (for example, in order to sell them) violates this prohibition. The Rambam, however, disagrees, as we have learned earlier (see *Section* II, *The Source of the Mitzvah*). In his view, a person who makes idols for others does not violate this prohibition, but does violate other prohibitions, such as Mitzvah 214 and Mitzvah 39.

Determine Mastery

REVIEWING KEY INFORMATION

1. Why is making an idol a sin, even without worshipping it?
2. At what exact point does a person violate this prohibition when he hires someone else to make an idol?
3. Can one use the money he received for making an idol?
4. Does a person have to sacrifice his life rather than make an idol? Why?
5. Why is it forbidden to make an image of Hashem?

CRITICAL THINKING

1. Explain the phrase עשו סיג לתורה and what it has to do with this mitzvah.
2. In what ways is the Torah unusually strict in regard to עבודה זרה? Give examples.

MITZVAH 28

Dedicated by

Menachem and Mariam Lieber and Family

Do Not Bow Down to an עבודה זרה

מצוה

איסור השתחואה לעבודה זרה

לעלוי נשמת

ר' יחזקאל

בן ר' משה זאב ז"ל

ר' יוסף בער

בן ר' יעקב לייב ז"ל

MITZVAH 29

Do Not Worship an עבודה זרה

מצוה

כט

איסור עבודה לעבודה זרה

A NEGATIVE COMMANDMENT מצות לא תעשה

MITZVAH 28

איסור השתחואה לעבודה זרה

Do Not Bow Down to an עבודה זרה

THE MITZVAH

A person is not allowed to bow down to an עבודה זרה*, or serve an* עבודה זרה *in any of the ways that Hashem is served in the* בית המקדש.

A NEGATIVE COMMANDMENT מצות לא תעשה

MITZVAH 29

איסור עבודה לעבודה זרה

Do Not Worship an עבודה זרה

THE MITZVAH

A person is not allowed to serve an עבודה זרה *in the way it is worshipped by its followers.*

Keywords

- לֹא תִשְׁתַּחֲוֶה
- וְלֹא תָעָבְדֵם
- נִסּוּךְ
- קִטּוּר
- בְּמֵזִיד
- בְּשׁוֹגֵג
- הַתְרָאָה
- נַעֲשֶׂה וְנִשְׁמַע
- הֵיכָל
- בָּא לְטַהֵר
- מְסַיְּעִין

SECTION I

Introduction to the Mitzvah

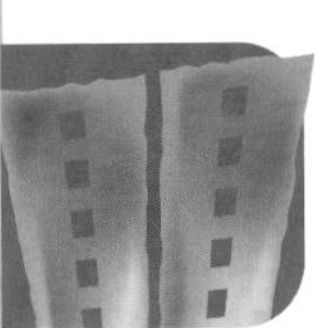
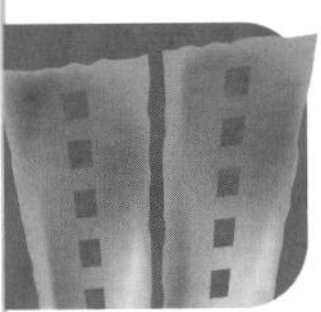

Hashem knew that worshipping עבודה זרה would be a major stumbling block for a human being. Therefore, He gave us many מצוות prohibiting the worshipping of other "gods." Four of them are in the עשרת הדברות.

The first one, Mitzvah 26, לֹא יִהְיֶה לְךָ אֱלֹהִים אֲחֵרִים עַל פָּנָי, prohibits us from believing that any other "god" exists besides Hashem. The second, Mitzvah 27, לֹא תַעֲשֶׂה לְךָ פֶסֶל וְכָל תְּמוּנָה, prohibits us from making an idol or image to worship. The third prohibition, Mitzvah 28, לֹא תִשְׁתַּחֲוֶה לָהֶם, prohibits us from serving an עבודה זרה in the way we would serve Hashem in the בית המקדש. The final prohibition, Mitzvah 29, וְלֹא תָעָבְדֵם, forbids us to worship any עבודה זרה in the manner that it is usually worshipped, even if that manner is disgusting and degrading.

Hashem and Bnei Yisrael share a very special relationship. When Hashem gave us the Torah, He made us His special people, a nation forever obligated to carry out His will. In turn, Hashem has forever linked His Name with the Jewish people.

When a person serves עבודה זרה, he breaks the special bond he shares with Hashem. In fact, states the *Pachad Yitzchak* (*Chanukah*), no other sin, no matter how much that sin goes against the will of Hashem, completely denies the special relationship between Hashem and Bnei Yisrael like the sin of worshipping עבודה זרה.

Mitzvah 28 and Mitzvah 29 are very similar in their laws and concepts. Although they are two separate מצוות, they have many similarities. Therefore, we present them together.

Why is the sin of עבודה זרה worse than any other aveirah?

A person is not allowed to bow down to an עבודה זרה or serve an עבודה זרה in any of the ways that Hashem is served in the בית המקדש.

The Source of Mitzvah 28

SECTION II

לֹא תִשְׁתַּחֲוֶה לָהֶם

שמות כ:ה פרשת יתרו

Do not bow down to them

Even though the פסוק here states, לֹא תִשְׁתַּחֲוֶה לָהֶם, *Do not bow down to them*, the Torah prohibits not only bowing before an עבודה זרה, but also serving it in any of the other ways in which Hashem was served in the בית המקדש.

We learn this from the פסוק in שמות (22:19) which states: זֹבֵחַ לָאֱלֹהִים יָחֳרָם בִּלְתִּי לַה׳ לְבַדּוֹ, *One who slaughters to the "gods" shall be destroyed, only to Hashem alone.* Chazal derive from the last three words of the פסוק, בִּלְתִּי לַה׳ לְבַדּוֹ, *only to Hashem alone,* that any form of worship that was done for Hashem is included in this prohibition. Such worship is reserved only for Hashem, and must not be directed toward any other.

~ *Sanhedrin* 60b

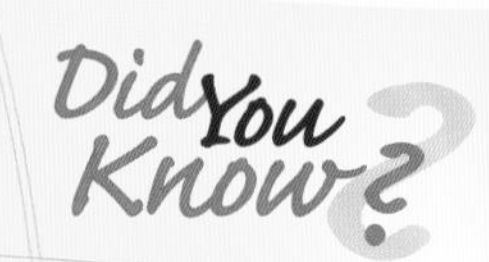

Singing or playing music before any idol is included in this prohibition, because that is how the Leviim served Hashem in the בית המקדש.

~ *Meiri* to *Sanhedrin* 60b

What is the Torah prohibiting us to do in this mitzvah, and from where do we learn this?

A person is not allowed to serve an עבודה זרה in the way it is worshipped by its followers.

SECTION II

The Source of Mitzvah 29

וְלֹא תָעָבְדֵם

שמות כ:ה פרשת יתרו

And do not worship them

Mitzvah 29 differs from Mitzvah 28 in that this mitzvah prohibits serving an עבודה זרה in whatever manner it is customarily served by its followers.

The Rambam explains that a different way of worship was invented for each עבודה זרה. No two idols were worshipped in the same way.

Therefore, בית דין had to be familiar with the various forms of worship so that they would know if a person violated this prohibition and was liable to punishment.

~ *Rambam*, הלכות עבודה זרה 3:2

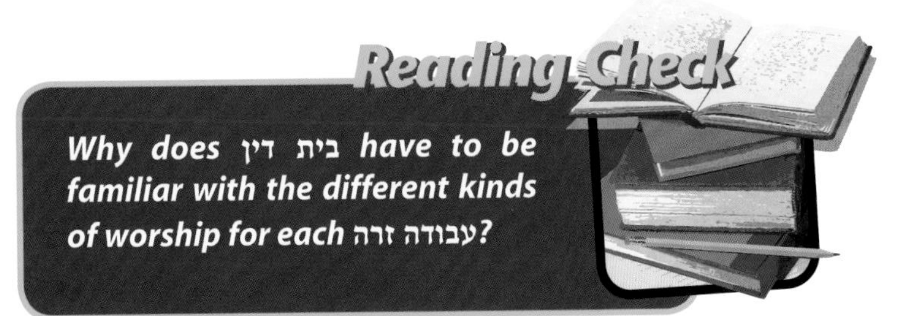

Why does בית דין have to be familiar with the different kinds of worship for each עבודה זרה?

A person is not allowed to bow down to an עבודה זרה or serve an עבודה זרה in any of the ways that Hashem is served in the בית המקדש.

The Laws of Mitzvah 28

SECTION III

1. An עבודה זרה is any object or being (such as an angel or a star) which the worshipper believes has free-will and its own power, or a statue or image representing it. This prohibition applies even if a person believes that Hashem is the Supreme God and intends to honor Him by worshipping one of His creations.

2. This prohibition forbids four specific types of worship that were done in the בית המקדש: (a) הִשְׁתַּחֲוָאָה — Bowing; (b) שְׁחִיטָה — Slaughtering an animal as an offering; (c) נִסּוּךְ — Pouring any liquid, or sprinkling blood of a sacrifice, as an offering; and (d) קִטּוּר — Burning food or incense as an offering.

3. A person who serves an עבודה זרה in one of these four ways has violated this prohibition even if the עבודה זרה is not usually served in that way.

4. These four services are prohibited whether they are performed in the presence of the עבודה זרה or not, as long as it is clear that the person's intention was to worship the עבודה זרה.

5. A person who serves an עבודה זרה has violated this prohibition, even if he never verbally declared that the עבודה זרה was his god, but believed it in his heart. A person also violates this prohibition if he declares an עבודה זרה to be his god, even if he does not serve it.

6. A person who violates this prohibition deliberately (בְּמֵזִיד) is sentenced to death by stoning (סְקִילָה) by בית דין, if he was properly warned (הַתְרָאָה) and there were two valid witnesses. A person who violates this prohibition inadvertently (בְּשׁוֹגֵג) must offer a קרבן חטאת.

7. A person must sacrifice his life rather than worship עבודה זרה. This is one of the three מצוות that a Jew must not violate, even if it means giving up his life (יֵהָרֵג וְאַל יַעֲבוֹר).

8. This commandment applies to both men and women, in all places and at all times. As a general rule, all of the Torah's prohibitions (מצוות לא תעשה) apply equally to men and women.

9. Non-Jews are forbidden to worship idols as well, since the prohibition against idolatry is one of the שֶׁבַע מִצְוֹת בְּנֵי נֹחַ.

A person is not allowed to serve an עבודה זרה in the way it is worshipped by its followers.

SECTION III The Laws of Mitzvah 29

1. An עבודה זרה is any object or being (such as an angel or a star) which the worshipper believes has free-will and its own power, or a statue or image representing it. This prohibition applies even if a person believes that Hashem is the Supreme God and intends to honor Him by worshipping one of His creations.

2. Showing honor or love for an idol, such as hugging or kissing it, is prohibited even if it is not part of the customary worship of that idol. However, such acts are not punishable by בית דין, unless they are customary acts of worship for that idol.

3. A person violates this prohibition even if he serves the idol in a demeaning or insulting way, if the idol is usually worshipped that way.

4. A person who serves an עבודה זרה has violated this prohibition, even if he never verbally declared that the עבודה זרה was his god, but believed it in his heart. A person also violates this prohibition if he declares an עבודה זרה to be his god, even if he does not serve it.

5. A person who violates this prohibition deliberately (בְּמֵזִיד) is sentenced to death by stoning (סְקִילָה) by בית דין, if he was properly warned (הַתְרָאָה) and there were two valid witnesses. A person who violates this prohibition inadvertently (בְּשׁוֹגֵג) must offer a קרבן חטאת.

6. A person must sacrifice his life rather than worship עבודה זרה. This is one of the three מצוות that a Jew must not violate, even if it means giving up his life (יֵהָרֵג וְאַל יַעֲבוֹר).

7. This commandment applies to both men and women, in all places and at all times. As a general rule, all of the Torah's prohibitions (מצוות לא תעשה) apply equally to men and women.

8. Non-Jews are forbidden to worship idols as well, as the prohibition against idolatry is one of the שֶׁבַע מִצְוֹות בְּנֵי נֹחַ.

Note: If the customary form of worship of a particular עבודה זרה is one of the four ways in which Hashem is served in the בית המקדש, then a person who worships that עבודה זרה violates both Mitzvah 28 and Mitzvah 29. (By believing that the עבודה זרה is a "god," he violates Mitzvah 26 as well.)

טוב טעם
Appreciating the Mitzvah

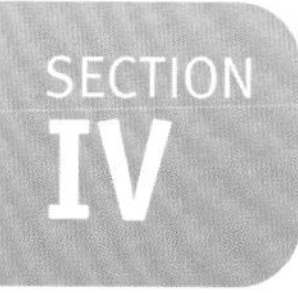

SECTION IV

A person is not allowed to bow down to an עבודה זרה or serve an עבודה זרה in any of the ways that Hashem is served in the בית המקדש.

Another Reason Why Bnei Yisrael Worshipped עבודה זרה

Throughout the ages, the nations of the world have abandoned Hashem and have turned to idols of wood and stone. Many times, Bnei Yisrael would follow these nations down the road to idolatry.

Didn't the people know that the idols were nothing more than wood and stone? Why would a person abandon Hashem, the One Who gave him life, to serve other "gods" that have no power at all?

The Gemara in *Sanhedrin* (63b) tells us that Bnei Yisrael were well aware that the idols were worthless and had no power. They ran to worship עבודה זרה only to throw off the yoke of Torah and be free from obeying the מצוות.

Bnei Yisrael's Loss Due to the עגל הזהב

R' Simai taught: When Bnei Yisrael said נעשה, "We will do" as Hashem says even before they said נשמע, "We will hear" what Hashem wishes us to do, six hundred thousand angels came and adorned each Jew with two crowns: one for נעשה and one for נשמע. But when Bnei Yisrael sinned by worshipping the עגל הזהב, twice that number of destructive angels descended and removed the crowns, as the פסוק states (שמות 33:6): וַיִּתְנַצְּלוּ בְנֵי יִשְׂרָאֵל אֶת עֶדְיָם מֵהַר חוֹרֵב, *The Children of Israel were stripped of their jewelry from Har Sinai.*

Reish Lakish said: Hashem will return the crowns to us in the future, as the פסוק states (*Yeshayah* 35:10): וּפְדוּיֵי ה' יְשֻׁבוּן וּבָאוּ צִיּוֹן בְּרִנָּה וְשִׂמְחַת עוֹלָם עַל רֹאשָׁם, *And the redeemed of Hashem will return, and they will come to Tzion with song, and eternal joy will be upon their heads.* This refers, explains Reish Lakish, to a joy that was long ago upon their heads — the crowns they received at Sinai.

~ see שבת 88a

Did You Know?

The Torah tells us that when Yitzchak Avinu grew old, his eyes became weak. The Medrash Tanchuma tells us one reason why this happened. Eisav's wives used to burn incense to their gods. The שכינה, which was always present in Yitzchak's house, departed because of the עבודה זרה. Yitzchak was very sad when this happened, and it pained him greatly to see this idol worship. Hashem caused Yitzchak's eyesight to fade so that he would not see what was happening and would not suffer any more.

~ *Medrash Tanchuma*, תולדות §8

A person is not allowed to serve an עבודה זרה in the way it is worshipped by its followers.

בא ליטהר מסייעין אותו

At the beginning of the era of the second בית המקדש, the אַנְשֵׁי כְּנֶסֶת הַגְּדוֹלָה, the *Men of the Great Assembly,* gathered together to decide how to strengthen Bnei Yisrael's Torah observance. They realized that one of the things that had caused the destruction of the first בית המקדש — the יצר הרע to worship עבודה זרה — was still causing Bnei Yisrael to sin.

The Gemara tells us that the חכמים cried out to Hashem and they said, "This is what caused many *tzaddikim* to be killed, destroyed the House of Hashem, and burned the היכל; it killed the righteous, exiled the Jews from their land, and still it dances among us! Hashem, did You give us this יצר הרע for any other reason than to reward us if we overcame it? If that is the case, then we do not want it. We would rather not have the יצר הרע and we will give up the reward!"

These great men were seeking Divine assistance on behalf of Bnei Yisrael, asking for help in getting rid of the terrible יצר הרע that was lodged in their hearts. They knew that בָּא לִטַהֵר מְסַיְעִין אותו, *If one comes to be purified* (to do sincere תְּשׁוּבָה), *Hashem assists him.*

They fasted three days and three nights, continuously praying to Hashem. Finally, a note fell down from Heaven with just one word upon it: אמת, *truth*. This word is the seal of Hashem. Just as a king of flesh and blood will sign a decree with his seal, Hashem signs His decrees with His seal. This told the חכמים that Hashem had accepted their prayers and would do as they had asked.

Hashem listened to their pleas and agreed to help Bnei Yisrael abandon their evil ways of worshipping false gods. That is how the אַנְשֵׁי כְּנֶסֶת הַגְּדוֹלָה were able to conquer the יצר הרע for עבודה זרה.

~ *Sanhedrin* 64a

Not only is it forbidden to worship an עבודה זרה, it is forbidden to appear to worship an עבודה זרה.

If a person is standing in front of an idol and he drops some coins, he may not immediately bend down while facing the idol to pick them up, lest it look like he is bowing to the idol. Rather, he should either turn around so that his back is to the idol, or he should turn sideways, and then bend down to pick up the coins.

~ see עבודה זרה 12a; *Tur* and *Shulchan Aruch, Yoreh Deah* 150:2

Living the Mitzvah

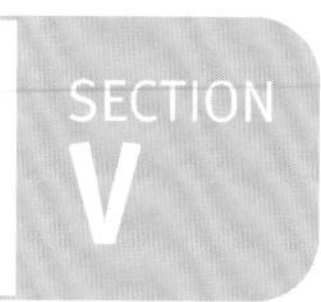

Eliyahu on Har HaCarmel

Achav, the son of Omri, sat on the throne of מלכות ישראל. He and his wife, Izevel, did evil in the eyes of Hashem and caused others to sin as well. In Achav's time, idolatry reached a new level. In addition to the various forces, spirits, and idols that had been worshipped until then, many people now began worshipping Baal.

During this time, Hashem sent the great Eliyahu HaNavi, a student of Achiyah HaShiloni, to try to influence Bnei Yisrael to do תְּשׁוּבָה. Eliyahu HaNavi wanted Bnei Yisrael to see the fallacy of worshipping idols and to fully return to Hashem, the One Who created and guides all that exists. He wanted them to see that idols like Baal have no power at all. He warned them time and again to abandon their idols and return to Hashem.

Eliyahu saw that the nation could not decide whether to follow Hashem or to turn to the Baal. He therefore wanted to discredit Baal once and for all. To accomplish this, Eliyahu challenged the priests of Baal to prove that Baal was the true god. He proposed a test. Both he and the priests of Baal would offer sacrifices. Whoever could bring down fire from Heaven to accept the sacrifice would thereby prove that his god was the true God. The priests readily accepted the challenge.

With Achav's consent, four hundred and fifty of the prophets and priests

A person is not allowed to bow down to an עבודה זרה *or serve an* עבודה זרה *in any of the ways that Hashem is served in the* בית המקדש.

of Baal gathered on Har HaCarmel, and many of Bnei Yisrael gathered to witness the test as well.

Eliyahu announced the stipulations of the challenge to the people: "I alone remain as a prophet of Hashem, and there are four hundred and fifty prophets of Baal. Let us be given two identical bulls. Let the priests of Baal choose one, prepare it for sacrifice and place it on their מזבח. I will prepare the other bull and place it on another מזבח. The priests will call out in the name of Baal, and I will call out in the Name of Hashem. Whoever sends down fire from Heaven to consume his sacrifice is the true God."

The people agreed to these conditions, and the challenge began.

The priests of Baal were given the first chance to bring down fire. They also had the advantage of numbers, for there were four hundred and fifty of them, while Eliyahu stood alone on the other side.

Of course, the priests of Baal knew that they had no chance of winning this contest. They knew Baal would not answer their prayers, for it was just a piece of stone. They therefore concocted a plan.

Chiel, a friend of Achav's, was very upset with this challenge. He was the person who started to rebuild the city of Yericho. Yehoshua had decreed that whoever rebuilt the city of Yericho would be punished; his oldest son would die when the foundation was laid, and his youngest son would die when the city was finished. This is exactly what happened to Chiel. All his sons had died, yet he steadfastly refused to believe that it was because of Yehoshua's words. He firmly believed that it was all due to "natural causes." Now he had a chance to prove that Baal was the religion everyone should be following.

Once the terms of the test were announced, Chiel built a מזבח on Har HaCarmel that was hollow inside. He himself climbed inside holding a torch. When he received the signal from the priests of Baal, he would push the fire onto the מזבח and the priests would claim that Baal had sent it.

With their plan in place, the priests of Baal prepared their bull for sacrifice. They began to pray, "Oh, Baal, answer us!" But there was no answer. In fact, everything was still. Hashem made the entire area silent;

no animals made a sound, no wind blew, nothing stirred. In this way, the priests could not claim that Baal had responded with a natural call, or that Baal had said to cancel the test. Now, they could make no such claim, so they continued to cry out to Baal to answer them and send down a fire.

They tried to create fire through magic, but Hashem did not allow any of their magic spells to work. They were beginning to get nervous. They wondered why Chiel was not doing his part. The priests began to jump up and down on their מזבח, during their worship, trying to signal Chiel to light the fire.

At noontime, Eliyahu began to mock them. "Speak louder," said Eliyahu. "Maybe Baal is talking, or chasing his enemies. Or perhaps he is asleep!"

The priests screamed louder. They performed all their rituals. They cut their flesh with swords and spears until blood was dripping from their bodies. But still, Baal did not answer them. Something had gone very wrong with their plan. Where, they wondered, was Chiel?

Chiel, who had been hiding inside the priests' מזבח, could not fulfill

A person is not allowed to bow down to an עבודה זרה or serve an עבודה זרה in any of the ways that Hashem is served in the בית המקדש.

his part of the plan. Hashem punished Chiel for his past sins, and also prevented him from causing a great חילול ה'. If fire had appeared on the Baal's מזבח, the people would have believed in Baal. Therefore, Hashem sent a poisonous snake to kill Chiel. It crawled into Chiel's hiding spot and bit him, and Chiel died.

The priests and prophets of Baal remained on Har HaCarmel all afternoon, crying and praying, performing their rites and "prophesizing," until the time of the afternoon offering. But there was no response from Baal.

Eliyahu then called to the people to come closer to him and give him their attention. Eliyahu built a מזבח and dug a trench all around it. He then prepared his bull for sacrifice. He commanded some people to fill four jugs with water and to pour the water over the bull and over the wood. He told them to do this three times until the water drenched the wood, and even filled up the trench that he had dug.

Eliyahu then offered up a prayer to Hashem: "Hashem, God of Avraham, Yitzchak, and Yisrael, today it will be made known that You are God in Yisrael and I am Your servant; and by Your word, I have done all these things. *Aneini, Hashem, aneini* — Answer me, Hashem, answer me! Let this people know that You, Hashem, are the true God; and You will turn their hearts back to You."

As soon as Eliyahu finished his prayer, a fire of Hashem descended from the Heavens and consumed the sacrifice, the wood, the rocks of the מזבח, the earth surrounding it, and even the water that filled the trench.

All the people who were there saw this tremendous נס, and together as one they cried out, "*Hashem Hu HaElokim! Hashem Hu HaElokim!* Hashem, He is the true God! Hashem, He is the true God!"

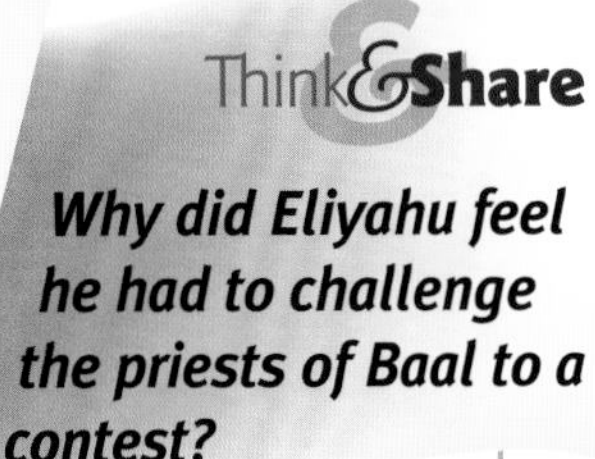

Think&Share

Why did Eliyahu feel he had to challenge the priests of Baal to a contest?

The priests of Baal, defeated and disgraced, tried to escape, but Eliyahu instructed the people to chase them and round them all up. All the priests of Baal were caught and put to death.

As a result of Eliyahu's triumph, Bnei Yisrael did תְּשׁוּבָה and returned to Hashem.

Living the Mitzvah

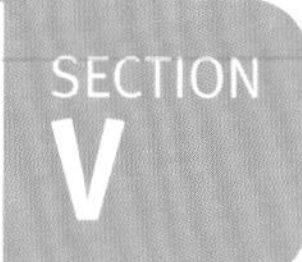

SECTION V

Chana and Her Seven Sons

Antiochus, ruler of the Syrian-Greeks, was quite pleased with himself. Here he was, the most powerful ruler in the world. Yet one thing irked him. There was one country in his kingdom, a tiny country, that was giving him trouble. The people in that country would not be subjugated. Indeed, those Jews were causing him so much trouble. They refused to take on the Greek customs and way of life. No matter what he did, they would not forsake their faith to follow his. True, there was a group of Jews here, an individual there, who freely accepted the Hellenistic lifestyle and were very happy to cast off their Judaism. But they were the minority.

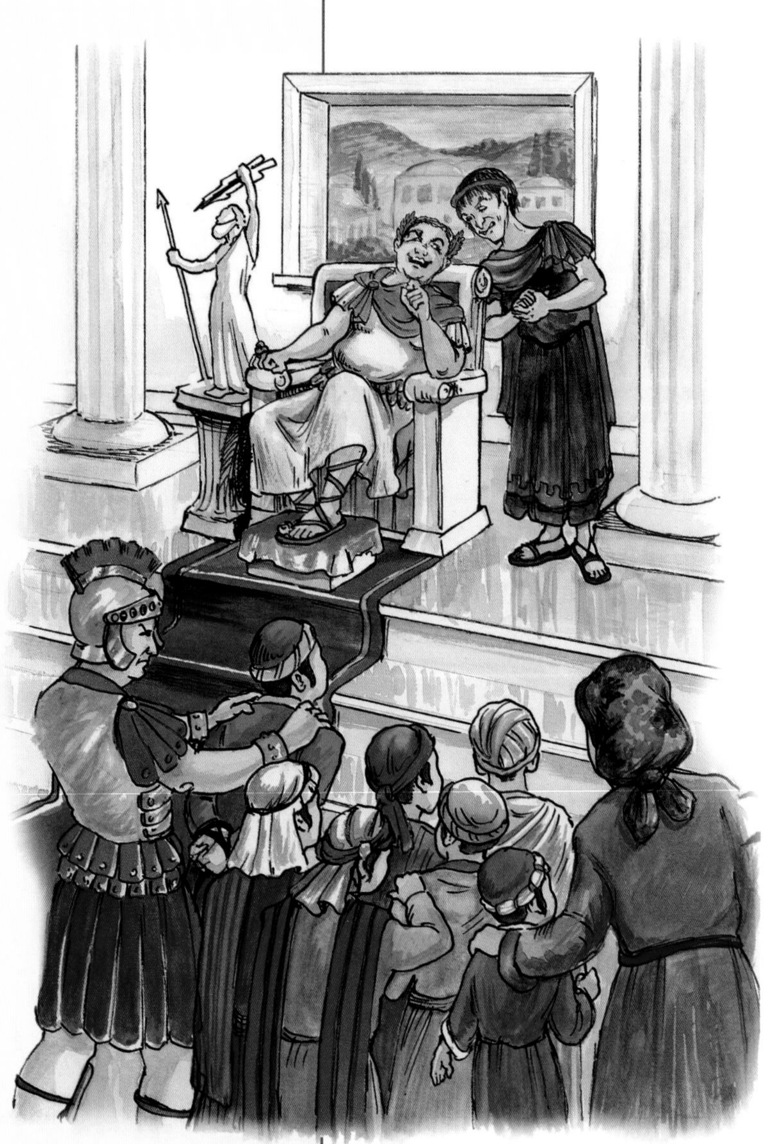

The sculptures depicted do not represent actual idols that were worshipped. They are included merely to present the reader with an understanding of the events which took place in the story.

However, most of the Jews in that small country of Eretz Yisrael were fighting him every step of the way. Some of them were even openly disobeying his edicts. He had issued specific decrees for the Jews — they were not to keep שבת, they were not to circumcise their sons, and they were not to keep track of the new moons — designed to distance them from their religion. But it just wasn't enough. He had to think of something more drastic.

Antiochus pondered and finally came up with a decree that he was certain would crush the Jews once and for all:

A person is not allowed to serve an עבודה זרה in the way it is worshipped by its followers.

From now on, Bnei Yisrael could only serve Antiochus' idols, they were not allowed to keep kosher, and they must reject their Torah. Whoever followed this edict would live, and whoever refused would be put to death.

Antiochus, very pleased with himself, appointed his trusted soldier, Philip, as governor over Judea. Philip's first act as governor was to initiate the new decree. Antiochus left everything in Philip's hands and prepared to return to his capital.

As Antiochus was setting out on his journey, he received a message from Philip: The new decree had already resulted in disobedience and arrest. They had just arrested a woman and her seven sons, and they were going to make an example of them.

Antiochus could not resist; this was going to be too good to miss! He turned his whole entourage around and returned. He wanted to personally preside over the proceedings.

The woman, Chana, and her seven sons were brought before Antiochus and Philip. The death sentence was pronounced upon them. But, lest anyone think that Antiochus was not a "compassionate human being," he would give each of them one more chance to save himself.

They brought the eldest son forward. "Bow to the idol," commanded Antiochus, pointing at the statue next to him.

The son replied, "It says in the Torah, 'I am Hashem, your God.' I will not bow to another." Antiochus commanded his men to kill the boy, in front of his mother and his brothers.

Next they brought the second son forward. "Bow to the idol," commanded Antiochus again.

The boy just stood there and said, "It says in the Torah, 'You shall not have other gods before Me.' No! I will not bow down to your idol!" They took him and slaughtered him before his family.

The third son was brought before the king. Again the king commanded, "Bow to the idol."

And again, the boy refused, saying, "It says in the Torah, 'One who sacrifices to a "god" shall be utterly destroyed.' I will not bow down to your idol!" Antiochus had him put to death.

The fourth son was brought and the scene repeated itself yet again. The boy refused to bow down, saying, "It says in the Torah, 'Do not bow down to another god.'" He, too, was murdered.

The fifth son was brought forward and he, too, refused, saying, "It says in the Torah, 'Hear Israel! Hashem is our God, Hashem is One.'" The sixth son said, "It says in the Torah, 'You will know this day and you will take it to heart that Hashem, He is the only God in Heaven above and on the earth below; there is no other.'" Both of them were executed.

Chana's youngest son was brought forward. He was a young boy, still a baby in his mother's eyes. Antiochus wanted desperately to convince this child to bow down to his idol. The fact that an entire family was standing firm against him was highly embarrassing for Antiochus. He should be able to convince at least one member to do as he commanded. Perhaps the littlest one would do what he wanted.

"Bow down to the idol," he commanded the small boy.

The little boy looked up at the king and said, "It says in the Torah, 'You have singled out Hashem today to be your God, and He has singled you out to be His people.' We have sworn to Hashem that we will never forsake Him for another god, and He has promised

A person is not allowed to serve an עבודה זרה in the way it is worshipped by its followers.

us that He will never forsake us for another nation. No, I will not bow down to your idol. I will go to my death as did my brothers before me."

Antiochus said to the boy, "You do not have to die like your brothers. In fact, you do not even have to bow down to this idol at all. I will throw my signet ring down and all you have to do is pick it up for me. You won't be bowing down, but it will look that way to all who are watching."

The little boy replied, "If you are so concerned for your own honor that you are willing to fool people into thinking that I listened and heeded your command, how much more concern must I have for the honor of the Holy One, Blessed is He! I will not do as you command."

As they led the boy away to his death, Antiochus looked at Chana. "He is your last son. Do you want him to be killed as well? Talk some sense into him. Convince him to do as I have asked and pick up my ring, and he and you shall both go free."

Chana called after the guards, "Give him to me. Let me kiss him, and perhaps I can talk to him."

She took her son and wrapped him in her arms. She kissed him and comforted him. Not once did she try to convince him to do as Antiochus wanted. Instead, she told him, as if she were speaking to all of her sons, "My sons, go and tell your father, Avraham: You bound a sacrifice on one altar, but I bound sacrifices on seven altars!" And with that, they took her last son away and his soul joined those of his brothers.

As her last son's soul ascended to the Heavens, Chana, too, joined her sons in the ultimate sacrifice in the honor of Hashem. As she died, a בת קול, *a Heavenly voice,* cried out, אֵם הַבָּנִים שְׂמֵחָה, *The mother of the children rejoices.*

Why didn't the last son agree to pick up the signet ring? He wasn't bowing to an idol, he was just picking up the king's jewelry!

Expand Your Knowledge

Question: In times of old, it was customary to bow to an important person when greeting him. Is a Jew allowed to greet a person in this manner if the person is wearing or displaying an idol or image?

As we have already learned (see *More on the Mitzvah*), Chazal prohibited many activities because they ***appear*** to be idol worship. Therefore, some Rishonim say that a Jew cannot bow to a person wearing an idol or the like around his neck, even if there will be terrible consequences if he does not bow down. Even though the Jew would not be bowing to the man in order to worship the idol around his neck, but rather because he must show respect for him, it would appear as if he was worshipping the idol, and he is forbidden to bow.

Other Rishonim disagree, and maintain that if the person is a man of importance, and it is obvious to everyone that the reason someone would bow to him is because of who he is and not what he is wearing, then one is allowed to bow to him, though it is better to avoid doing so if possible.

Challenge: Find an instance in Tanach where a person did bow down to idol worshippers, even though they had a form of עבודה זרה with them; and find another instance where a person did not bow down in similar circumstances.

Determine Mastery

REVIEWING KEY INFORMATION

1. What is the difference between Mitzvah 28 and Mitzvah 29?
2. What is an עבודה זרה?
3. How did Bnei Yisrael react to the outcome of Eliyahu's challenge?
4. What decrees did the wicked Antiochus enact against the Jews?

CRITICAL THINKING

1. Explain: בָּא לְטַהֵר מְסַיְּעִין אותו. How can we apply this concept in our daily lives?
2. Why did the אַנְשֵׁי כְּנֶסֶת הַגְּדוֹלָה feel that it was the right time to ask Hashem to remove the יצר הרע for עבודה זרה?

לע"נ

מוה"ר צבי יהודה ע"ה

בן מוה"ר אברהם יצחק לאו"ט

נפטר כ"ח מנחם אב

מצוה

MITZVAH 30

Do Not Make a Vain Oath in Hashem's Name

איסור שבועת שוא

MITZVAH **30**

איסור שבועת שוא

Do Not Make a Vain Oath in Hashem's Name

THE MITZVAH

It is forbidden to make a vain oath in Hashem's Name in any language.

- לֹא תִשָּׂא
- לַשָּׁוְא
- כִּנּוּי
- רַחוּם
- אֶרֶךְ אַפַּיִם
- שְׁבוּעָה
- וְחִלַּלְתָּ
- בְּרָכָה לְבַטָּלָה
- צְרִיכָה

SECTION I

Introduction to the Mitzvah

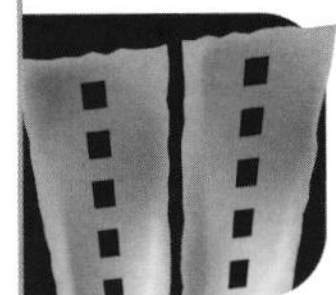

The stranger was dressed in laborer's clothes, a sack slung over his back. No one in the village knew his true identity. He was the king. He ruled over a vast empire and this village was hundreds of miles from his capital city. He had come to this village to see what the villagers thought of him and his government.

When he arrived at the center of the village, he entered an inn and sat down at a table in the corner. From his vantage point, he could see and hear everything that was happening in the inn. At that moment, three men came in and took seats near the fire and were quickly served a meal.

"I swear in the name of the king," exclaimed the first man, "that this bread is quite stale!"

"I swear in the name of the king," cried out the second, "that this chicken was cooked last year!"

"I swear in the name of the king," yelled out the third, "that this is the best cup of coffee I've had all week!"

From the corner where he sat, the king had heard everything and could not contain himself any longer. He rose to his full height and all could see his regal bearing. "I am your king," he said, "and I see now how little respect you have for me. I see how you use my name in vain! What disgrace you bring to my honor!"

The של"ה הקדוש tells us that a king of flesh and blood would not tolerate the use of his name for pointless oaths. Can we expect the King of kings to tolerate such a thing?

When someone uses Hashem's holy Name in a vain oath, he shows complete disregard for Hashem's honor.

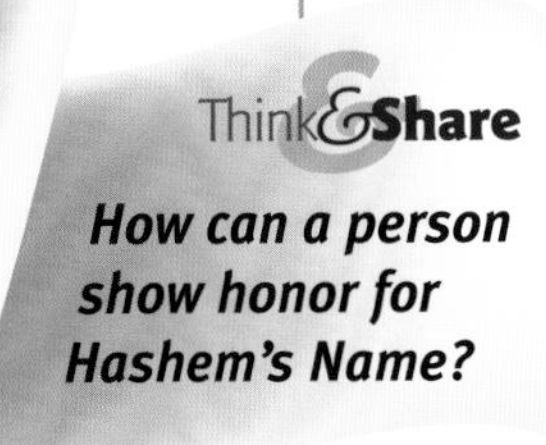

Think&Share

How can a person show honor for Hashem's Name?

The Source of the Mitzvah

SECTION II

לֹא תִשָּׂא אֶת שֵׁם ה' אֱלֹקֶיךָ לַשָּׁוְא

שמות כ:ז פרשת יתרו

Do not take the Name of Hashem, your God, in vain

In this prohibition, the Torah uses the words, שֵׁם ה' אֱלֹקֶיךָ, *the Name of Hashem, your God*. This comes to forbid using any of Hashem's Names in a vain oath. It also forbids using any one of Hashem's מידות (referred to as כִּנּוּיִים) in a vain oath. An example of a כִּנּוּי would be the term הרחום, *He Who is Merciful,* or ארך אפים, *He Who is Slow to Anger*. Even making a vain oath with a reference to Hashem in another language (for example, using the word God in a vain oath) is prohibited.

~ *Rambam,* הלכות שבועות 2:2-4

Did You Know?

A person who makes a vain or meaningless oath not only violates the prohibition of לא תשא*, but also violates Mitzvah 432, the mitzvah to fear Hashem. The mitzvah to fear Hashem includes treating Hashem's Name with reverence and respect, and refraining from mentioning it in vain.*

~ *Temurah* 4a

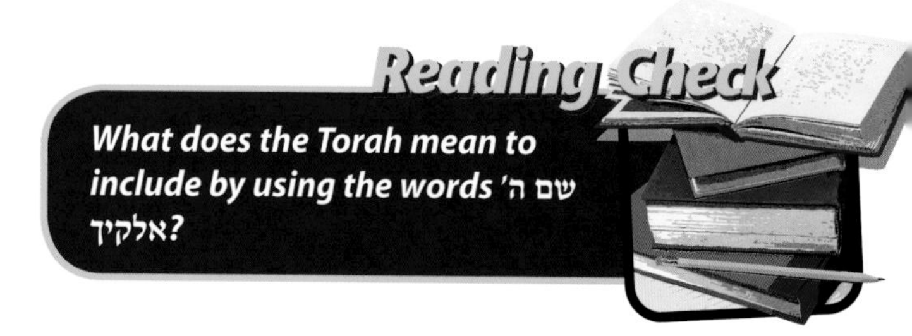

What does the Torah mean to include by using the words שם ה' אלקיך?

It is forbidden to make a vain oath (שבועת שוא) in Hashem's Name in any language.

SECTION III

The Laws of the Mitzvah

1. A שְׁבוּעָה, *oath,* accomplishes one of the following: (a) It obligates a person to do or not do a certain act; for example, "I swear to do [or not to do] such and such..."; or (b) It attests to the truth of a statement; for example, "I swear that yesterday I paid..." If an oath does not accomplish either of these things, then it is a vain oath.

2. There are four types of שְׁבוּעוֹת שָׁוְא, *vain oaths*: (a) an oath contradicting an obvious fact, such as swearing that a stone is gold; (b) an oath attesting to an obvious fact, such as swearing that a stone is a stone; (c) an oath to do something impossible, such as swearing not to eat and drink for a month; and (d) an oath not to perform a mitzvah or to violate a prohibition, such as swearing to do *melachah* on שבת or not to put on *tefillin.* (This would be a vain oath, because at the time of מתן תורה the Jewish people made a collective שְׁבוּעָה to fulfill the מצוות. This שְׁבוּעָה is binding on all Jews in all generations. Therefore any שבועה to violate a mitzvah contradicts this שְׁבוּעָה and cannot take effect [שֶׁכְּבָר מֻשְׁבָּע וְעוֹמֵד מֵהַר סִינַי].)

3. A שְׁבוּעָה is created through a verbal declaration. If a person answers "Amen" to an oath said by someone else on his behalf, it is as if he made the oath himself.

4. This prohibition applies to both men and women, in all places and at all times. As a general rule, all of the Torah's prohibitions (מצוות לא תעשה) apply equally to men and women.

5. If a person who violates this prohibition received proper warning (הַתְרָאָה) and witnesses testified that he violated it, then he receives מַלְקוּת. This prohibition is one of the exceptions to the rule that one does not receive מַלְקוּת for a לא תעשה whose violation does not involve a physical action (לָאו שֶׁאֵין בּוֹ מַעֲשֶׂה).

Note: For the separate prohibition to make a false oath, see Mitzvah 227.

טוב טעם
Appreciating the Mitzvah

A Vain Oath Is a Direct Insult to Hashem

A person who regularly makes vain oaths shows his lack of respect and total disregard for Hashem's honor. He is compared to a person who serves עבודה זרה.

Chazal tell us: The עשרת הדברות begin with אָנֹכִי ה׳ אֱלֹקֶיךָ, *I am Hashem, your God,* which teaches us belief in Hashem. They then continue with לֹא יִהְיֶה לְךָ אֱלֹהִים אֲחֵרִים, *You shall not recognize other gods,* which forbids idolatry. Then the עשרת הדברות continue with לֹא תִשָּׂא אֶת שֵׁם ה׳ אֱלֹקֶיךָ לַשָּׁוְא, *You shall not take the Name of Hashem, your God, in vain.* What is the connection between לֹא תִשָּׂא and the first two commandments?

The Torah is teaching us that a person who regularly makes vain oaths is considered as if he had worshipped idols. For just as we must fear Hashem Himself, and not give the honor we owe Him to another by worshipping idols, so must we fear Hashem's Name and treat it with the utmost respect. One who uses Hashem's Name in vain profanes that Name, as it is written (ויקרא 19:12), לֹא תִשָּׁבְעוּ בִשְׁמִי לַשָּׁקֶר וְחִלַּלְתָּ אֶת שֵׁם אֱלֹקֶיךָ, *You shall not swear falsely in My Name, and thereby desecrate the Name of your God.*

~ *Tanna D'Vei Eliyahu Rabbah* 26:14

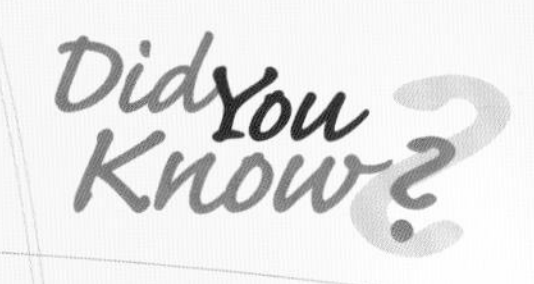

According to some authorities, even mentioning Hashem's Name in vain, without making an oath, is considered a violation of לא תשא.

~ see *Ramban* and *Rabbeinu Bachya* to שמות 20:7; see also *Sefer HaChinuch* §30

The Maharal states that in a way, this sin is even worse than idol worship. He explains this with the following משל:

In a certain kingdom, two cities rebelled against the king. One city immediately chose another person to be king, while the second city did not choose another ruler, but declared that the real king was an impostor. The king considered the second city to have committed a worse offense than the first city. The first city, although they chose someone else to be their king, did not

It is forbidden to make a vain oath (שבועת שוא) in Hashem's Name in any language.

attack the king directly. The second city, however, insulted the king directly by declaring him to be fake, although they did not choose another ruler.

In the same way, a person who worships עבודה זרה has committed a terrible sin but has not attacked Hashem directly. But a person who uses Hashem's Name in meaningless and vain oaths disgraces Hashem directly by showing that although he knows that there is a true God, he has no respect for Him.

~ *Maharal,* תפרת ישראל §39

Bringing Honor to Hashem

The primary reason for this mitzvah is that an oath that serves no purpose, even if it is true, shows thoughtless disrespect for Hashem's honor. We are not to use Hashem's Name casually.

A person who truly accepts Hashem as his Master will always be careful to speak His Name only in connection to matters of *kedushah* (or when he is required to do so by בית דין), and even then, only when absolutely necessary. He would never use his Master's Name regarding unimportant matters.

~ עקידת יצחק §45

When we observe this commandment, we develop an awareness of Hashem and the holiness of His Name. We become aware that Hashem's Name should only be used with awe and respect.

If we are careful in our speech to treat Hashem's Name with the proper respect and honor, we bring honor to Hashem.

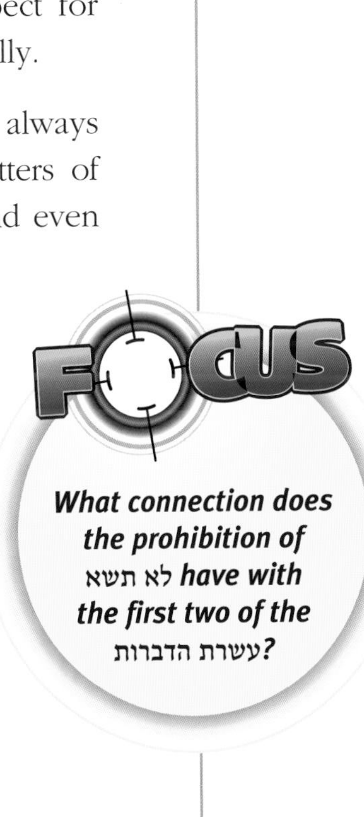

Living the Mitzvah

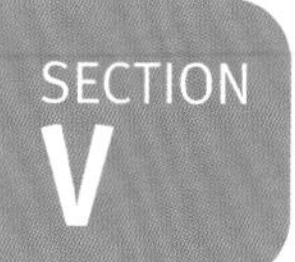

SECTION V

The Crooked Cane

Although the mitzvah of לֹא תִשָּׂא אֶת שֵׁם ה' אֱלֹקֶיךָ לַשָּׁוְא *forbids a person to make a vain oath, it is also a warning against making any false oath, for when a person makes a false oath, he is also using Hashem's Name in vain. This idea is found in the Gemara (*שבועות *37a) which teaches that before a defendant would swear in* בית דין*, the judges would attempt to frighten him into testifying truthfully by saying, "Know that the whole world shook when Hashem said at Har Sinai,* לֹא תִשָּׂא אֶת שֵׁם ה' אֱלֹקֶיךָ לַשָּׁוְא. *The following story is based on the Gemara in Nedarim (25a), which relates the story of a person who attempted to trick* בית דין *with a "true" oath.*

Shimon was in desperate need. His business was not doing well at all. His last failed venture had cost him almost everything he owned. He was lucky to still have a roof over his head and the clothes on his back. His family wasn't starving, yet. He was just getting by, but only barely. Shimon and his family would not survive much longer without help. He knew that he would have to swallow his pride and seek a loan.

He was very anxious as he approached Reuven. Reuven was his last resort. As it was, Shimon had no collateral, and no

It is forbidden to make a vain oath (שבועת שוא) in Hashem's Name in any language.

business plan to recoup his losses. He would have to start from scratch and rebuild his business from the ground up.

Reuven greeted his visitor warmly. He was not a rich man, but he was comfortable enough that perhaps he could help Shimon out. To Shimon's immense relief, Reuven agreed to loan him the sum of money he needed. The men shook hands and the deal was struck.

Months passed. Shimon's business began to prosper once again. Hashem had granted him success and more than enough money to support his family. He began to make plans for expanding his business.

Reuven, however, was not happy at all. He knew that Shimon was doing well, but the time had come to repay the loan and Shimon had not even contacted him. He sent messages to Shimon, but Shimon ignored them. Finally, having no choice, Reuven contacted the בית דין, and Shimon was summoned to court.

On the day that his case went to trial, Shimon appeared in the courtroom wearing expensively tailored clothes and leaning on a beautifully carved walking stick. He stood before the court and declared, "I don't know why I was summoned to this court. I have paid Reuven every last *dinar* that I owed him."

Reuven stared at Shimon in disbelief. "You never gave me anything!" Reuven shouted. "The loan was due, and I sent you message after message. I heard about your success, and assumed that you would come to me to repay the loan. How dare you stand here and lie before Hashem and בית דין!"

"But my dear Reuven," exclaimed Shimon, "I am not lying at all. I have repaid you. Perhaps your memory is playing tricks on you."

The great Amora and head of the בית דין, Rava, looked at the two men. He turned to Shimon and said, "In order for your claim to be believed, you must make an oath stating that you did indeed give Reuven the money."

Shimon did not hesitate. He immediately agreed, and a Sefer Torah was brought for Shimon to hold while he made his שבועה. Shimon turned to Reuven and held out his cane.

"Would you please hold my cane for me while I make the oath?" he asked pleasantly. Reuven, still upset and getting angrier by the minute, took the cane from Shimon and held it while Shimon swore his שבועה.

It is forbidden to make a vain oath (שבועת שוא) in Hashem's Name in any language.

As Shimon swore in the Name of Hashem that he had given the money to Reuven, Reuven became so incensed that he took the beautifully carved cane and smashed it over a table.

To everyone's astonishment, the cane split open and money came pouring out of it. As Reuven somehow knew it would, when it was counted, the money equalled the amount Shimon owed him!

Shimon had hoped to get out of paying back the loan, so he had thought of this plan. When the time came to swear that he had given Reuven the money, Reuven would be holding the cane with the money inside. At the moment that Shimon made his oath, he would have indeed given Reuven the money he owed him! Shimon thought that this would not only free him from paying back the loan, but would also save him from having to make a false oath. However, when the cane broke, his plot was uncovered.

To prevent such trickery, Chazal decreed that whenever בית דין orders a person to take an oath, they must specifically inform him that בית דין is accepting the oath according to the court's understanding of the person's words, and not according to what the person means when he says the words of the oath. בית דין was forced to put this safeguard into our judicial system to protect against those few who would not only lie, but use Hashem's Name to do it.

FOCUS

How is a false oath like a vain oath?

MITZVAH 25
MITZVAH 26
MITZVAH 27
MITZVAH 28
MITZVAH 29
MITZVAH 30
MITZVAH 31
MITZVAH 32
MITZVAH 33
MITZVAH 34
MITZVAH 35
MITZVAH 36
MITZVAH 37
MITZVAH 38

Expand Your Knowledge

An Unnecessary *Berachah*:

The Torah uses the words, לֹא תִשָּׂא אֶת שֵׁם ה׳ אֱלֹקֶיךָ לַשָּׁוְא, *Do not **take** Hashem's Name in vain.* But if the Torah wants only to forbid *swearing* in vain using Hashem's Name, why doesn't the פסוק state, לא תשבע בשם ה׳ אלקיך לשוא, *Do not **swear** using Hashem's Name in vain?* The use of the words לֹא תִשָּׂא is teaching us that this prohibition includes other situations in which a person might use Hashem's Name in vain. One instance in which we must be very careful, since it can be considered a violation of this prohibition, is reciting unnecessary ברכות.

A person may not recite a *berachah* for no reason (בְּרָכָה לְבַטָּלָה). A person also may not recite a *berachah* which is not needed (בְּרָכָה שֶׁאֵינָהּ צְרִיכָה).

An example of a בְּרָכָה לְבַטָּלָה is when a person recites a *berachah* on a drink, and a minute later recites another *berachah* for the same drink. An example of a בְּרָכָה שֶׁאֵינָהּ צְרִיכָה is when a person recites a *berachah* on a bowl of soup, knowing that he is going to have bread and will have to wash his hands and say the *berachah* of המוציא. His first *berachah* should not have been said. He should have washed first before sitting down to eat anything else.

The Gemara (ברכות 33a) states that a person who makes an unnecessary blessing violates the prohibition of לֹא תִשָּׂא. Some authorities (see, for example, *Rambam*, הלכות ברכות 1:15) maintain that the Gemara means that the person actually violated the Torah prohibition (מִדְּאוֹרַיְתָא) of לֹא תִשָּׂא, while others (see תוספות to *Rosh Hashanah* 33a ד״ה הוא) explain that the Gemara means that the person violates a Rabbinic prohibition (מִדְּרַבָּנָן) based on the לא תעשה of לֹא תִשָּׂא.

If a person recited a *berachah* and realized that it was an unnecessary one, he should immediately say ברוך שם כבוד מלכותו לעולם ועד.

If a person said ברוך אתה ה׳, and then realized that he should not be saying a *berachah*, he should finish with the words לַמְּדֵנִי חֻקֶּיךָ.

Determine Mastery

REVIEWING KEY INFORMATION

1. What is a כִּנּוּי? Can one use a כִּנּוּי in a vain oath?
2. An oath accomplishes one of two things. What are they?
3. What are the four types of vain oaths?
4. Why is swearing not to put on תפילין considered a vain oath?
5. Why, according to the Maharal, is one who makes a vain oath worse than one who worships עבודה זרה?
6. Why does the Torah use the words לא תשא and not לא תשבע?
7. How did Shimon think he was going to trick Reuven and the entire בית דין?

CRITICAL THINKING

1. What do we learn from the way the king felt when he heard the townspeople swearing in vain using his name?

Dedicated by

Lennie and Jessica Weiss and Family

Lincolnwood, Illinois

מצוה

MITZVAH 31

Sanctify the שבת with Words

מצות קידוש שבת בדברים

MITZVAH **31**

מצות קידוש שבת בדברים

Sanctify the שבת with Words

THE *MITZVAH*

We are commanded to sanctify the שבת by praising it with words that describe its unique and holy qualities, both when it begins (kiddush) and when it ends (havdalah).

- אוֹת
- זָכוֹר
- שָׁמוֹר
- רְבִיעִית
- מִצְוַת עֲשֵׂה שֶׁהַזְּמַן גְּרָמָא
- עֹנֶג
- פַּת
- חֲמַר מְדִינָה

SECTION I

Introduction to the Mitzvah

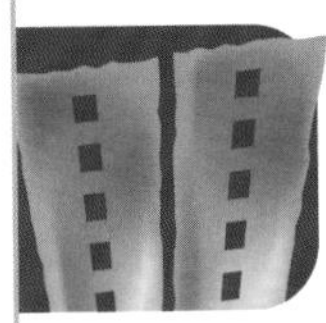

Have you ever seen a store without a sign above its front door? Without a sign, a person cannot tell if the store is opened or closed, or even what kind of business it is. Without a sign, it appears as if the store has gone out of business.

שבת, says the Chafetz Chaim, is called an אוֹת, *sign*, because it is the mitzvah which declares our belief in Hashem, Who created all that exists in six days, and rested on the seventh. שבת is the "sign" that proclaims who we are and Who we believe in.

שבת was given a special *kedushah* from Hashem. In this mitzvah, we are commanded to speak words of praise about שבת when it begins and when it ends. We do this by reciting *kiddush* and *havdalah*.

In the words of the Friday night *kiddush,* we declare that Hashem created the world and that שבת is a holy day. We also make mention of יציאת מצרים in *kiddush*. The miracle of יציאת מצרים shows that Hashem not only created the world, but that He also directs and controls all that happens.

When we say *kiddush,* we bear witness to all this: that Hashem created, and continues to guide and control the world, and that שבת is holy, and different than the other days of the week.

Havdalah, which we recite at the end of שבת, also sanctifies the שבת by highlighting the difference between שבת and all the other days of the week.

How does the text of havdalah show the holiness of שבת?

MITZVAH 25 · MITZVAH 26 · MITZVAH 27 · MITZVAH 28 · MITZVAH 29 · MITZVAH 30 · MITZVAH 31 · MITZVAH 32 · MITZVAH 33 · MITZVAH 34 · MITZVAH 35 · MITZVAH 36 · MITZVAH 37 · MITZVAH 38

The Source of the Mitzvah

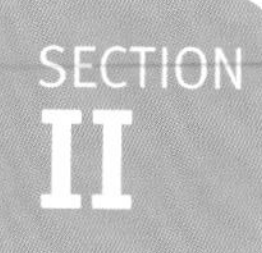

SECTION II

זָכוֹר אֶת יוֹם הַשַּׁבָּת לְקַדְּשׁוֹ

שמות כ:ח פרשת יתרו

Remember the שבת *day to sanctify it*

The word זכור means to remember. When the word זכור is used in the Torah, a person might think it means to remember something by just thinking about it. However, concerning the mitzvah of שבת, the Torah states elsewhere (דברים 5:12): שָׁמוֹר אֶת יוֹם הַשַּׁבָּת לְקַדְּשׁוֹ, *Guard the day of* שבת *to make it holy.* This פסוק already teaches us that we must have in mind the holiness of שבת. Therefore, the word זכור in this פסוק must be commanding us to declare the holiness of שבת verbally. We fulfill this mitzvah by reciting *kiddush* and *havdalah*.

~ תורת כהנים, בחקותי 1:3

Did You Know?

Although שבת *is holy in itself because Hashem made it so, we are nonetheless commanded to declare the* שבת *holy. Why? Because speaking of the holiness of* שבת *helps us to understand and appreciate how special it is. This reveals its holiness even more. Thus, the holier one makes* שבת*, the holier it becomes.*

~ see *Pri Tzaddik,* קדושת שבת §2

Reading Check

According to the* תורת כהנים*, what is the difference between* שמור *and* זכור*?

We are commanded to sanctify the שבת by praising it with words that describe its unique and holy qualities, both when it begins (kiddush) and when it ends (havdalah).

The Laws of the Mitzvah

1. A person is obligated to recite *kiddush* on Friday evening. If he began שבת early, he may recite *kiddush* before nightfall. If a person did not recite *kiddush* on Friday night, he can fulfill his *kiddush* obligation during the following day. However, he does not say the first section of *kiddush* (ויכולו), as it deals with Hashem's completion of the world's creation before שבת.

2. A person is obligated to recite *havdalah* at the end of שבת. If a person did not recite *havdalah* then, he may recite it up until (but not including) Tuesday evening.

3. By Torah law (מִדְּאוֹרַיְתָא), a person can fulfill this mitzvah with any words that contain praises of שבת. However, the אַנְשֵׁי כְּנֶסֶת הַגְּדוֹלָה established specific texts for *kiddush* and *havdalah*.

4. One must mention יציאת מצרים in *kiddush*.

5. A person can fulfill his obligation of *kiddush* or *havdalah* by listening to someone else say them. This applies only if he intends to fulfill his obligation this way and the person who is reciting the text has in mind to fulfill the listener's obligation.

6. *Kiddush* and *havdalah* should be recited over a cup of wine. The cup must contain at least a רביעית of wine. One must drink some of the *kiddush* and *havdalah* wine.

7. A person must recite *kiddush* where he intends to eat the שבת meal, and should begin the meal right after *kiddush*.

8. In addition to the *kiddush* at the beginning of שבת, which we are obligated in by Torah law (מִדְּאוֹרַיְתָא), Chazal instituted *kiddush* on שבת morning as well. This is fulfilled by simply reciting the *berachah* of בורא פרי הגפן over a cup of wine, and drinking some of the wine.

9. A person is obligated to recite *kiddush* and *havdalah* on יום טוב, *a holiday,* as well.

10. This mitzvah applies to both men and women, in all places and at all times. Although women are usually exempt from positive commandments that must be done at specific times (מִצְוַת עֲשֵׂה שֶׁהַזְּמַן גְּרָמָא), they are nevertheless obligated in *kiddush* and *havdalah*.

טוב טעם
Appreciating the Mitzvah
SECTION IV

שבת Instills *Emunah* in Hashem's Creation of the World

The fact that the world did not always exist, but was created by Hashem at the beginning of time, is one of the foundations of all of the Torah's principles. Therefore, every week we proclaim this fact by observing the שבת. Every basic article of *emunah* needs some kind of representation in order to instill the idea in our hearts and minds. שבת is the representation of the belief that Hashem created the world in six days and rested on the seventh. This fact is so fundamental that it calls for a *weekly* reminder to preserve its place of importance in our hearts and minds.

~ *Chinuch* §32, *Eitz HaChaim* 29:30

When a person recites the part of *kiddush* that recalls Hashem's creation of the world (ויכולו), the Torah considers him as if he had been a partner with Hashem in the creation of the world (שבת 119b). This is because by reciting these words, a Jew demonstrates his unwavering belief in their truth, as if he himself had witnessed creation and contributed to it.

~ see *Kol Bo* §35

שבת Is the Bride of Bnei Yisrael

שבת came before Hashem and complained, "Each of the other six days of the week has a match. Only I have no match."

Hashem told שבת, "Bnei Yisrael will be your match."

~ בראשית רבה 11:18

Each week, when we recite *kiddush,* we, Bnei Yisrael, welcome the שבת as a חתן welcomes his כלה under the *chuppah*. Just as a חתן welcomes his כלה with *kiddushin*, we sanctify the שבת with *kiddush*.

~ *Maharsha*, חדושי אגדות, *Bava Kamma* 32b

עונג שבת וכיבודה

Chazal tell us, "Fortunate is the person who honors the שבת; fortunate is he in this world and in עולם הבא."

~ *Zohar*, שמות 64a

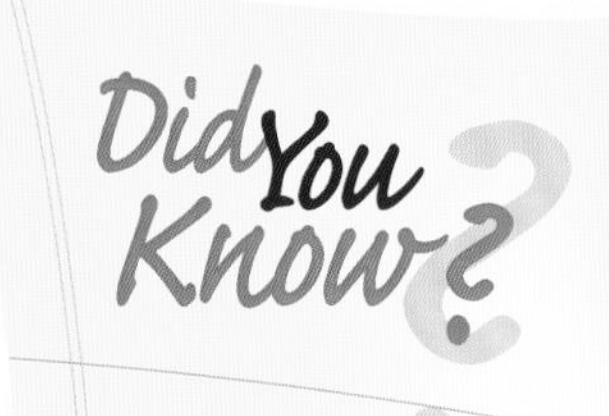

We light a candle when we recite havdalah to commemorate the first man-made fire that אדם הראשון lit on the first מוצאי שבת. In addition, Chazal instructed us to smell בשמים during havdalah to lessen our sadness at the departure of שבת.

~ *Pesachim* 54a; *Rambam*, הלכות שבת 29:29

We are commanded to sanctify the שבת by praising it with words that describe its unique and holy qualities, both when it begins (kiddush) and when it ends (havdalah).

The שבת is compared to a queen and we must honor it accordingly. Therefore, we are commanded to recite *kiddush* as the שבת begins, to welcome the visiting monarch, and to recite *havdalah* at the end of שבת, to bid farewell and accompany our important guest when she leaves.

~ see *Pesachim* 103a

Just as we would give a queen all sorts of honor, so too, we must give honor to the שבת Queen. In addition to greeting the queen, we would do other things to honor her, such as dress in fine clothing, set a beautiful table, and prepare delicious foods in her honor. For this reason, Chazal tell us to take delight and pleasure in the שבת, for that is honoring the day as well; as Yeshayah HaNavi tells us in the verse, וְקָרָאתָ לַשַּׁבָּת עֹנֶג לִקְדוֹשׁ ה׳ מְכֻבָּד, *You shall proclaim the* שבת, *'a delight', and the holy day of Hashem, 'honored'* (*Yeshayah* 58:13).

One honors the שבת with any act that demonstrates the importance of שבת. Some of these acts are performed in honor of the שבת before it arrives, such as preparing the שבת meals, cleaning the house, and bathing oneself. Some actions are performed on the שבת itself, such as wearing clean and elegant clothing and having candles lit at one's שבת meal. The Gemara (שבת 119a) tells us that the great Tannaim and Amoraim would salt fish, chop wood, and do other chores themselves in honor of שבת. We honor the שבת by taking pleasure in the day through special food and drink, learning Torah, enjoying the opportunity to rest from our labors, and enjoying being close to Hashem.

~ see *Tanna D'Vei Eliyahu Rabbah* 26:20

On Friday night, two angels escort a man home from shul, one good angel and one bad angel. If the man comes home and finds the candles lit, the table set, and the bed made, then the good angel says, "May it be the will of Hashem that it should be like this next שבת," and the bad angel is forced to answer "Amen." But if the man comes home and the house is not prepared for שבת, the bad angel says, "May it be the will of Hashem that it should be like this next שבת" and the good angel is forced to answer "Amen."

~ שבת 119b

More on the Mitzvah

All the money that a person spends to honor שבת is repaid to him by Hashem. Although the amount of money each person will have every year is decided on Rosh Hashanah, the money a person spends for שבת is not included; if he spends extra for שבת, he will receive more money than he was originally going to receive.

~ *Beitzah* 15b-16a

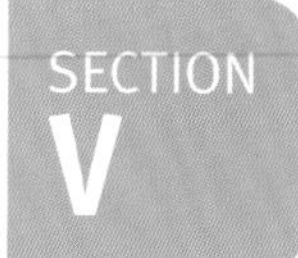

Living the Mitzvah

SECTION V

Rabbi Zakkai and His Mother

The Gemara (Megillah 27b) tells us of a discussion between Rabbi Zakkai and his disciples. Rabbi Zakkai's talmidim asked their very aged teacher what he had done in his life to merit living so long. Rabbi Zakkai listed three מצוות *in which he had always been especially careful, one being the mitzvah of kiddush. Rabbi Zakkai told his students, "I always recited the* שבת *kiddush over wine."*

Rabbi Zakkai was a great תלמיד חכם, always learning night and day. Surely, he was meticulous in his observance of all the מצוות, yet his extra diligence in the mitzvah of *kiddush* earned him long life.

It was very difficult for R' Zakkai to fulfill the mitzvah of reciting *kiddush* over wine, because he was extremely poor. But Rabbi Zakkai did not complain. He was happy to sit and learn Torah, and he was always thankful to Hashem for this privilege. His family had little or nothing in the way of food or possessions.

We are commanded to sanctify the שבת *by praising it with words that describe its unique and holy qualities, both when it begins (kiddush) and when it ends (havdalah).*

During the week, Rabbi Zakkai and his family would make do with only the barest necessities, so that any money left over could be used to buy wine for *kiddush*.

One Friday there was no money to buy even the smallest amount of wine. There was nothing of value in the house that he could sell for even a few coins. Rabbi Zakkai was very disappointed that he would not be able to recite *kiddush* over a cup of wine that night. After all, he had always been so careful to fulfill this mitzvah meticulously. It seemed that he would have no choice but to recite the *kiddush* over challah that night, as one does when no wine is available. But he accepted this as the will of Hashem and went to the בית המדרש to learn Torah.

The entire household was upset at this turn of events, especially Rabbi Zakkai's mother. She never complained about the poverty in the house; she was comforted by the fact that her son learned Torah day and night. She knew how scrupulous her son was when it came to the mitzvah of *kiddush*. She was determined to find a way to obtain some money to buy wine for *kiddush*. She looked through her things in order to find something of value which she might be able to sell, but anything of value was long gone.

Suddenly, she thought of something she could sell that might fetch a few coins; she would sell her scarf. In the days of the Tannaim and Amoraim, it was common for a married woman to cover her head with a scarf. Rabbi Zakkai's mother wanted to sell one of the scarves that she owned.

It was getting late, and שבת was coming soon. Quickly, Rabbi Zakkai's mother ran to the marketplace. She approached a peddler who was about to close his stall and practically begged him to buy her scarf. At first, the peddler did not want to deal with the woman. What would he do with another scarf? But finally he relented and agreed to buy it.

Rabbi Zakkai's mother did not even haggle over the price. She took what the peddler offered her and ran to the wine peddler. All she was able to buy with the paltry sum she had received for her scarf was the smallest bottle of wine. But it

We are commanded to sanctify the שבת by praising it with words that describe its unique and holy qualities, both when it begins (kiddush) and when it ends (havdalah).

was enough for *kiddush*. She hurried back home. The family was relieved and overjoyed that there would be wine for *kiddush*. They waited expectantly for Rabbi Zakkai to come home from shul.

When Rabbi Zakkai came home and saw the wine on the table, he was ecstatic. After he made *kiddush*, he asked each member of the family who it was that had found enough money to buy the wine. Rabbi Zakkai's mother did not say a word. But Rabbi Zakkai was a smart man. He noticed his mother was not wearing her usual scarf. Realizing what she had done, he praised her and blessed her, assuring her that Hashem would surely pay her back.

Indeed, she was paid back for her selflessness and her willingness to give up her only possession of any value so that her son would have wine for *kiddush*. Rabbi Zakkai's mother became very rich. Hashem rewarded her devotion to the mitzvah of *kiddush*, measure for measure. When she passed away, she left three hundred barrels of wine for her son to inherit. The family never again had to worry about having enough wine for *kiddush*.

The Gemara concludes by telling us that the *berachah* continued and multiplied, for when Rabbi Zakkai passed away, after a long, righteous life, he left his children three thousand barrels of wine.

Hashem granted Rabbi Zakkai long life and great wealth for keeping the mitzvah of *kiddush* with such dedication and devotion.

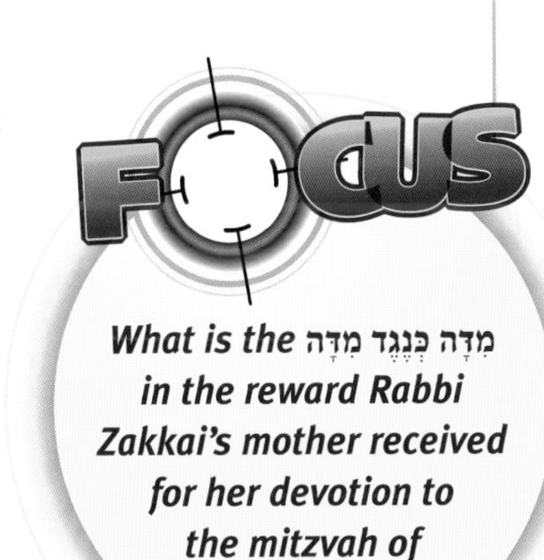

What is the מִדָּה כְּנֶגֶד מִדָּה in the reward Rabbi Zakkai's mother received for her devotion to the mitzvah of kiddush?

Expand Your Knowledge

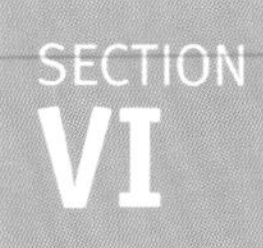

When Wine Cannot Be Used:

1

If a person does not have wine for קידוש on Friday night, or if he is not allowed to drink wine for medical reasons, and there is nobody there to make *kiddush* for him, how can he fulfill the mitzvah of *kiddush*?

There are two items that can be used in place of wine (or grape juice) in case of necessity: 1. פַּת, which includes anything upon which the ברכה of המוציא is said; and 2. חֲמַר מְדִינָה (literally: "wine of the country"), a drink that one might serve a guest to whom one wishes to show honor. There are different opinions as to which beverages are considered חֲמַר מְדִינָה.

2

Which is better to use, פַּת or חֲמַר מְדִינָה?

For the Friday night *kiddush,* פַּת is preferable to חֲמַר מְדִינָה. For the *kiddush* of שבת morning, the opposite is true. For *havdalah,* חֲמַר מְדִינָה may be used, but not פַּת.

Women Are Also Obligated in *Kiddush* and *Havdalah*

Both men and women are obligated in the לא תעשה of not performing *melachah* on שבת, and the law is that whoever is obligated in the לא תעשה of שבת is also obligated in the עשה of *kiddush* and *havdalah*.

Challenge:

Havdalah is recited twice on מוצאי שבת. When and why?

Determine Mastery

REVIEWING KEY INFORMATION

1. When one recites kiddush, to what is he testifying?
2. Which פסוק is the source for the mitzvah of קדוש שבת בדברים?
3. How do we fulfill the mitzvah of זָכוֹר אֶת יוֹם הַשַּׁבָּת לְקַדְּשׁוֹ every שבת?
4. What conditions must be met in order for a person to fulfill the mitzvah of kiddush or havdalah by listening to another person say them?
5. What do we learn from the פסוק: וְקָרָאתָ לַשַּׁבָּת עֹנֶג לִקְדוֹשׁ ה׳ מְכֻבָּד?

CRITICAL THINKING

1. Why do we mention יציאת מצרים in kiddush?
2. Why are the expenses for שבת not budgeted for a person on Rosh Hashanah?

INVESTIGATE & INQUIRE

1. Hashem rewards and punishes מִדָּה כְּנֶגֶד מִדָּה, measure for measure. One example of this is the ten מכות that Hashem brought upon the Egyptians in מצרים. Can you match a corresponding aveirah to each of the ten מכות?

לעילוי נשמת אבינו

ר' בנימין ליב בן ר' יחיאל ריאס ז"ל

שהיה נשמתו דבוק בקדושת השבת כל ימי חייו

Drs. Craig and Jackie Reiss and Family

Chesterfield, Missouri

מצוה

32

MITZVAH

Do Not Perform Forbidden Labor on שבת

איסור עשיית מלאכה בשבת

MITZVAH **32**

איסור עשיית מלאכה בשבת

Do Not Perform Forbidden Labor on שבת

THE MITZVAH

On שבת, a Jew is forbidden to perform any of the thirty-nine labors, the ל״ט מלאכות, that were performed during the construction of the Mishkan (these are called אבות), or any melachah (labor) that resembles one of the thirty-nine (these are called תולדות).

- ל״ט מְלָאכוֹת
- תּוֹלָדוֹת
- וַאֲמָתְךָ
- מְלֶאכֶת מַחְשֶׁבֶת
- גְּרָמָא
- חִלּוּל שַׁבָּת
- שִׁיעוּר
- מֵעַיִן

SECTION I

Introduction to the Mitzvah

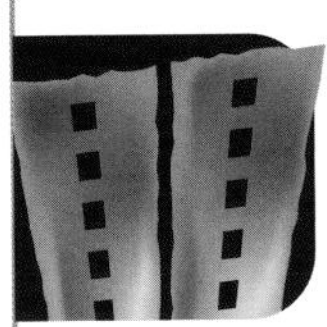
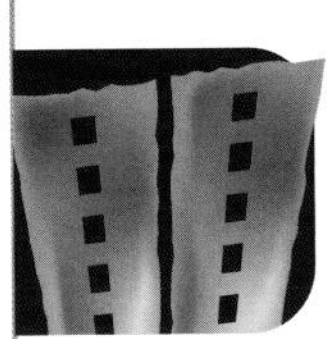

Yaakov hurriedly pulled the gate down over his storefront and locked up. His non-Jewish competitor across the street yelled to him, "Yaakov, where are you going so early?"

Yaakov answered, "It's Friday afternoon. I'm going home to prepare for שבת. I'll see you on Sunday."

"On Sunday?" repeated his rival. "If you don't open your store tomorrow, you won't have any business left on Sunday. All your customers will come to shop in my store tomorrow."

"Tomorrow is שבת," explained Yaakov. "We Jews cannot work on that day. But don't you worry about my business. It will be just fine. My customers will be back come Sunday morning. Not only will my business not suffer because I close my store on שבת, it will prosper!"

In the עשרת הדברות, the Torah states (שמות 20:9-10): שֵׁשֶׁת יָמִים תַּעֲבֹד וְעָשִׂיתָ כָּל מְלַאכְתֶּךָ וְיוֹם הַשְּׁבִיעִי שַׁבָּת לַה׳ אֱלֹקֶיךָ לֹא תַעֲשֶׂה כָל מְלָאכָה, *Six days you shall work and do all your labor, and the seventh day is* שבת *to Hashem, your God; you shall not do any labor.* The Torah links the true observance of שבת to the stopping of all work. Why do we have to stop all our work in order to keep the שבת?

When we don't do *melachah* on שבת, we show that in addition to believing that Hashem created the world in six days and rested on the seventh day, we also believe that all the work we do, and everything we accomplish during the six days of work, is all from Hashem. None of it comes from our own power.

When a Jew keeps שבת and does not go out to earn his livelihood, he is declaring his belief that Hashem is the One who takes care of him, and that all the money he did earn during the previous six days is from Hashem.

By observing שבת and not performing any *melachah*, we are showing that we know Hashem is our Master and Creator, and that He sustains all of Creation.

Why does doing melachah on שבת contradict what שבת represents?

The Source of the Mitzvah

SECTION II

וְיוֹם הַשְּׁבִיעִי שַׁבָּת לַה' אֱלֹקֶיךָ
לֹא תַעֲשֶׂה כָל מְלָאכָה אַתָּה וּבִנְךָ וּבִתֶּךָ
עַבְדְּךָ וַאֲמָתְךָ וּבְהֶמְתֶּךָ וְגֵרְךָ אֲשֶׁר בִּשְׁעָרֶיךָ

שמות כ:י פרשת יתרו

And the seventh day is שבת to Hashem, your God;
you must not do any labor — you, and your son,
and your daughter, your slave, and your maidservant,
and your animal, and your convert who is within your gates

The פסוק tells us: לֹא תַעֲשֶׂה כָל מְלָאכָה, *You must not do any labor.* What work, exactly, is the Torah telling us not to do on שבת?

In פרשת ויקהל (שמות 35:1-20), the Torah places the list of items needed to construct the Mishkan immediately following another command not to perform forbidden labor on שבת. From this, Chazal derived that all tasks that were needed for the construction and setup of the Mishkan are forbidden on שבת. These acts make up the ל"ט מלאכות that are forbidden on שבת.

~ see *Rashi* to שבת 5a ד"ה לדגלי מדבר

Did You Know?

The prohibition against doing melachah on שבת also appears in ספר ויקרא as part of a passage that teaches the laws of the ימים טובים. This is to teach us that observing the festivals and holidays is as important as keeping שבת.

~ see *Rashi* to ויקרא 23:3

Reading Check

From where do we know which מלאכות are forbidden on שבת?

On שבת, a Jew is forbidden to perform any of the thirty-nine מלאכות (labors) that were performed during the construction of the Mishkan (these are called אבות), or any melachah (labor) that resembles one of the thirty-nine (these are called תולדות).

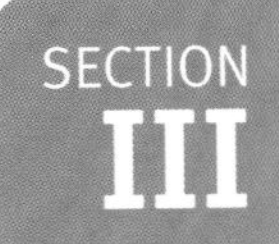

SECTION III The Laws of the Mitzvah

1. By Torah law (מִדְּאוֹרַיְתָא) a person violates this prohibition only if he performs a calculated, purposeful act (מְלֶאכֶת מַחְשֶׁבֶת). In order for an act to be considered calculated and purposeful, all of the following must be true:

a. It is the act that one intended to perform. This excludes two types of acts:

(1) Something he did not mean to do at all (מִתְעַסֵּק). An example of מִתְעַסֵּק is: If a person intended to pick a fig off a tree and his hand slipped and he tore a grape off a nearby vine instead, he has not violated this prohibition מִדְּאוֹרַיְתָא.

(2) If a person intentionally performed an act that is not a *melachah*, but a *melachah* was performed as a *result* of this act, he has not violated this prohibition מִדְּאוֹרַיְתָא. For example: If a person drags a chair across a yard, the legs of the chair will sometimes dig holes in the ground. Although digging holes of this type is a *melachah* (חוֹרֵשׁ), since the person did not intend (אֵינוֹ מִתְכַּוֵּן) to dig holes, but only to move the chair, he has not violated this prohibition.

There is, however, an important exception to this rule. If the chair that the person is dragging is so heavy that it will ***definitely*** dig holes in the ground, then the one who drags it is liable even if he did *not* intend to dig the hole. A case such as this one is called a פְּסִיק רֵישֵׁיהּ, which means "cut off its head"; just as a bird whose head is cut off will surely die, an act that will *surely* result in a *melachah* is forbidden, even if the person did not intend to do the *melachah*.

b. The act serves a constructive purpose, rather than being destructive (מְקַלְקֵל). For example: If a person tears a garment and ruins it, he has not violated this prohibition מִדְּאוֹרַיְתָא.

c. The act must be permanent in some way, and not an act that is not meant to last. For example: If a person wrote his name on a fogged windowpane or built a house out of blocks, he has not violated this prohibition מִדְּאוֹרַיְתָא.

d. The act is performed for the reason a person would normally perform it. For example: A person usually digs a hole because he needs the hole. If, however, he dug a hole, but only because he needed the dirt, he has not violated this prohibition מִדְּאוֹרַיְתָא.

e. The act is performed in its usual manner. For example: If a person carries something from his house into the street in his mouth or on his foot, he has not violated this prohibition מִדְּאוֹרַיְתָא.

It must be noted, however, that many acts that are not מְלֶאכֶת מַחְשֶׁבֶת *are still forbidden Rabbinically* (מִדְּרַבָּנָן).

2. In order to be liable מִדְּאוֹרַיְתָא, a person must perform a *melachah* directly. One who indirectly causes a *melachah* to occur (גְּרָמָא) has not violated the Torah prohibition (מִדְּאוֹרַיְתָא). For example: It is forbidden to extinguish a fire. However, if a person surrounds a fire with barrels of water, so that the fire will burn the barrels and release the water, which will in turn extinguish the fire, he has not violated this prohibition מִדְּאוֹרַיְתָא.

3. חִלּוּל שַׁבָּת, desecrating the שבת, is one of the worst sins. Chazal say that חִלּוּל שַׁבָּת is as serious as violating the entire Torah.

A person who deliberately (בְּמֵזִיד) performs a *melachah* on שבת that is forbidden מִדְּאוֹרַיְתָא in the presence of two valid

On שבת, a Jew is forbidden to perform any of the thirty-nine מלאכות (labors) that were performed during the construction of the Mishkan (these are called אבות), or any melachah (labor) that resembles one of the thirty-nine (these are called תולדות).

witnesses, after having received proper warning (הַתְרָאָה), is liable to execution by stoning (סְקִילָה).

If a person performs a *melachah* בְּמֵזִיד but was not warned properly beforehand, or if the act was not seen by two valid witnesses, he is not punished by בית דין. However, he is liable to כָּרֵת, meaning that Hashem will shorten his life.

A person who performs a *melachah* on שבת inadvertently (בְּשׁוֹגֵג) must bring a קרבן חטאת. בְּשׁוֹגֵג means either that he did not realize it was שבת or that he didn't know the act he performed was forbidden on שבת.

4. Many מלאכות require a specific minimum measure (שִׁעוּר) in order to make a person who performs them liable to the death penalty. For example: The minimum שִׁעוּר for weaving (אוֹרֵג) is weaving two threads, and the minimum שִׁעוּר for sewing (תּוֹפֵר) is two stitches. Performing less than the required measure, however, is still forbidden.

5. It is forbidden to instruct a non-Jew to perform *melachah* for you on שבת (אֲמִירָה לְעַכּוּ"ם). This is a Rabbinic decree (מִדְּרַבָּנָן).

6. Chazal forbade many activities on שבת because they resemble מלאכות or because doing them might lead a person to perform a *melachah* מִדְּאוֹרַיְתָא.

7. This prohibition applies to both men and women, in all places and at all times. As a general rule, all of the Torah's prohibitions (מצוות לא תעשה) apply equally to men and women.

טוב טעם
Appreciating the Mitzvah

שבת Commemorates the World's Creation

By observing שבת, we show the world the truth: that Hashem created the world from nothing (יֵשׁ מֵאַיִן), that He did so in six days, and on the seventh day, He rested.

When we observe שבת, and remember the creation of the world, we also remember the One who created it. שבת causes us to think about the greatness and the true majesty of our Creator, Who, just by speaking, with no physical action, called everything into existence.

~ *Radvaz,* טעמי המצוות §91

A Reminder of יציאת מצרים

When the עשרת הדברות are repeated in פרשת ואתחנן, the Torah teaches us that keeping שבת is a זֵכֶר לִיצִיאַת מִצְרָיִם, *a remembrance of the Exodus from Egypt.*

In Mitzrayim, Bnei Yisrael were not in control of their activities or their time. They were slaves, always subject to the decrees and whims of their masters. But when they left Mitzrayim, they were finally free to live as they wished. It was at that point, right after leaving Mitzrayim, that Hashem gave Bnei Yisrael the mitzvah of שבת. They became free men, no longer servants of a king of flesh and blood. They became Hashem's servants, able to devote their time to His service.

Being free to serve Hashem was a direct result of יציאת מצרים. Therefore, שבת is truly a זֵכֶר לִיצִיאַת מִצְרָיִם.

~ *Chinuch* §32; *Ramban,* דברים 5:14, citing *Moreh Nevuchim*

A Special Time with Hashem

שבת is a special gift to us from Hashem. The Gemara (*Beitzah* 16a) states that Hashem told Moshe Rabbeinu: I have a wonderful gift in My treasure house called שבת, and I wish to give it to the Jewish people. The Medrash elaborates that Hashem told Bnei Yisrael that the שבת was more dear to Him than all the other מצוות.

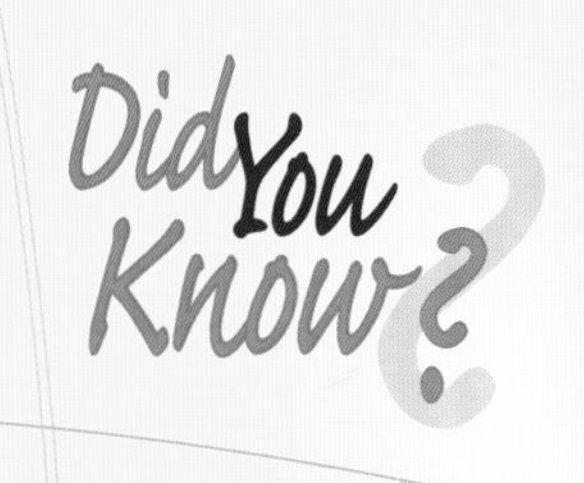

In Mitzrayim, when Moshe asked Pharaoh to give Bnei Yisrael one day a week on which to rest, Moshe asked for the seventh day of the week. Later, when Bnei Yisrael were given the mitzvah of שבת, Moshe rejoiced, for the day that he had asked that Bnei Yisrael be given to rest became our holy שבת. This is one reason why we say in שחרית on שבת morning, יִשְׂמַח מֹשֶׁה בְּמַתְּנַת חֶלְקוֹ.

~ אבודרהם השלם p. 170; שמות רבה 1:28; *Seder HaYom,* סדר קידוש של שבת

On שבת, a Jew is forbidden to perform any of the thirty-nine מלאכות (labors) that were performed during the construction of the Mishkan (these are called אבות), or any melachah (labor) that resembles one of the thirty-nine (these are called תולדות).

Hashem also says that if we merit to keep the שבת, He will consider it as if we have kept all the מצוות.

~ see שמות רבה 25:12, דברים רבה 4:4

שבת is a special time of closeness between Hashem and Bnei Yisrael, His chosen nation. The fact that Hashem gave us a day of rest on the same day that He rested shows the world how special we are. On שבת, Hashem prefers our company to that of His angels.

~ *Ohr Zarua*, שבת §42

The Talmud Yerushalmi (שבת 15:3) states that שבת was given to Bnei Yisrael so that they may spend time in the study of Torah. The pursuit of a livelihood usually occupies most of a person's time during the workweek. Therefore, Hashem designated one day a week during which we are required to refrain from mundane activities, allowing us to refresh our souls through the study of Torah.

~ עקידת יצחק §55

מעין עולם הבא

A person who refrains from doing *melachah* on שבת is living as אדם הראשון did in גן עדן, before the first *aveirah*. When אדם הראשון was in גן עדן, Hashem provided all his needs, and he did not have to make even the slightest effort. After Adam sinned, however, Hashem decreed that, בְּזֵעַת אַפֶּיךָ תֹּאכַל לֶחֶם, *With the sweat of your brow you shall eat bread* (בראשית 3:19). But every שבת, that decree is suspended; all work becomes unnecessary. This frees us to toil in Torah and מצוות.

~ *Pri Tzaddik*, בא §10

The radiance of שבת is מֵעֵין עוֹלָם הַבָּא, a hint of what we will experience in עולם הבא if we keep the Torah and מצוות. עולם הבא will be like a day that is completely שבת, for there will be no work or labor. Bnei Yisrael will sit and enjoy the closeness of the שכינה.

~ see ברכות 17a

Why is one who desecrates the שבת compared to an idol worshipper?

MITZVAH 25
MITZVAH 26
MITZVAH 27
MITZVAH 28
MITZVAH 29
MITZVAH 30
MITZVAH 31
MITZVAH 32
MITZVAH 33
MITZVAH 34
MITZVAH 35
MITZVAH 36
MITZVAH 37
MITZVAH 38

Living the Mitzvah

The Rabbi and the Lion

Rabbi Masoud Refael Alfasi was a great tzaddik and תלמיד חכם. *He was born and raised in Fez, Morocco, in the second half of the 17th century. His piety and greatness were known to all of Fez, and Rabbi Alfasi would have been very content to live out his life there, except for one thing: he longed to see Eretz Yisrael. Finally, Rabbi Alfasi decided to make the trip.*

In those days, before planes, cars, or even proper roads, the trip from Morocco to Eretz Yisrael was a long and difficult one, crossing deserts filled with all kinds of dangers.

Nevertheless, Rabbi Alfasi decided to join a caravan heading east toward Eretz Yisrael. The caravan consisted of non-Jewish traders and travelers, headed by a well-traveled Arab guide. All the travelers were riding the "ships of the desert," as camels are known, since they can travel for great distances in the desert because of the water they have stored inside them. Rabbi Alfasi approached the leader, and bought a place in the caravan. He was given his own "ship of the desert," and he took his place in the caravan.

Rabbi Alfasi knew that the trip would be a long one, and that he would not reach his destination before שבת. He approached the caravan leader and explained, "I am Jewish, and I cannot work or travel on the שבת. Please make camp before sundown on Friday until after nightfall on Saturday. I will make it well worth your while."

The caravan leader's eyes glinted greedily as he saw the money Rabbi Alfasi was offering him. "Don't worry, Rabbi," said the guide as he pocketed the money, "I am sure it won't be a problem. By Friday, we will all be in need of some rest."

On שבת, a Jew is forbidden to perform any of the thirty-nine מלאכות (labors) that were performed during the construction of the Mishkan (these are called אבות), or any melachah (labor) that resembles one of the thirty-nine (these are called תולדות).

The caravan set out and began its long journey. Slowly, the trees, the houses, and the people receded from view, and the land became barren and empty. All around them was sand, and above them, a burning sun beat down upon their heads. In the distance they could hear the growls of jackals, hyenas, and other wild animals.

In the afternoon they reached an oasis, where they enjoyed a small rest from the dangers and discomforts of the desert. After the short rest, they set out again.

So passed the first day, and the second day, and the third, the fourth, and the fifth; each day filled with the same long, uncomfortable, and frightening journey, broken up with short breaks and little sleep.

On the sixth day, Friday, the process repeated itself yet again. Rabbi Alfasi was wondering when the caravan leader was going to call a halt and stop the caravan for שבת. But the hours continued to pass, and they kept riding.

Finally, as the hour was getting late, Rabbi Alfasi approached the leader and asked him, "When are we stopping? It is almost sundown. We made a deal, you and I. I must stop traveling before sundown."

The caravan guide looked at Rabbi Alfasi as if he was insane. "We are not stopping here in the middle of nowhere," said the guide. "We will continue to ride until we reach the city of Tunis. And you will ride like everyone else, otherwise you will be left here at the mercy of the desert and all its inhabitants."

Rabbi Alfasi looked the guide in the eye and announced, "I will not ride on שבת. I will not desecrate the שבת. I will remain here. And if you will not fulfill your end of the bargain, I will remain here alone!"

The leader just laughed at him and walked away, shaking his head. Some of the other travelers laughed as well, and still others tried to dissuade Rabbi Alfasi from staying in the desert all alone. But Rabbi Alfasi remained firm in his decision; he would not be מְחַלֵּל שַׁבָּת, and if that meant staying in the desert all alone, so be it!

The caravan continued on its way without Rabbi Alfasi. As the afternoon drew to a close, Rabbi Alfasi took a stick and drew a circle in the sand. Inside the circle, he laid out the provisions he had brought for שבת; his

wine, his challah, and some other food. He recited Minchah, and then קבלת שבת. As night fell, he recited Maariv and then prepared for *kiddush*.

Suddenly, there was a roar. Rabbi Alfasi looked up. Coming straight at him was a huge lion, his wild mane blowing in the cool desert wind. Closer and closer, the lion approached. But just as the lion reached the circle Rabbi Alfasi had drawn, he stopped dead in his tracks, and calmly laid himself down right outside the circle!

Rabbi Alfasi was frightened and amazed at the same time. After several long moments, he went on to recite *kiddush*. He washed his hands and ate his challah, and still the lion just sat there. He ate his meal, and said ברכת המזון, and still the lion remained in place.

Rabbi Alfasi understood that the lion had been sent by Hashem, not to hurt him, but to protect him. With a feeling of immense gratitude to his Creator, and without fearing that the lion would devour him, Rabbi Alfasi went to sleep.

No harm came to Rabbi Alfasi during the night. All the creatures that would have hurt or killed Rabbi Alfasi did not dare approach him while the king of beasts was standing watch over him.

In the morning, when Rabbi Alfasi awoke, the lion was still lying there. Rabbi Alfasi prayed, ate his meal, and then spent the rest of the day learning Torah. שבת passed very peacefully, and when the time came, Rabbi Alfasi recited Maariv and then *havdalah*.

On שבת, a Jew is forbidden to perform any of the thirty-nine מלאכות (labors) that were performed during the construction of the Mishkan (these are called אבות), or any melachah (labor) that resembles one of the thirty-nine (these are called תולדות).

As soon as שבת was over, the lion got up and moved closer to Rabbi Alfasi. He crouched down again, his front legs extended, and shook his mane. Rabbi Alfasi understood the lion's message; the lion wanted Rabbi Alfasi to ride him! Quickly, he gathered up his belongings and approached the lion. He carefully climbed onto the lion's back. As soon as he was settled on top of the lion, it took off in the direction of the caravan.

The lion and the Rabbi reached the city of Tunis even before the caravan did. The people were terrified when a lion came flying through the city, but they were astonished to see Rabbi Alfasi riding it. Rabbi Alfasi called out to them, "Do not be afraid. No harm will come to you." He then dismounted. The people stared, openmouthed, as Rabbi Alfasi thanked the lion, picked up his belongings, and headed for the local inn. The lion gave a mighty roar in return, turned around, and raced out of the city the way it had come.

When the caravan finally arrived in Tunis, everyone was talking about the Rabbi who rode into town on a lion. The caravan guide and fellow travelers were even more astounded when they found out that it was none other than their Rabbi Alfasi, whom they had left all alone in the middle of the desert.

They ran to Rabbi Alfasi and asked him to tell them the entire story. When they had heard the tale from beginning to end, the leader threw himself down in front of Rabbi Alfasi and begged his forgiveness. He also gave Rabbi Alfasi back the money he had been given to stop the caravan for שבת. His fellow travelers also begged Rabbi Alfasi to forgive them. "Great is the God Who watches over His people from on High," they cried, "and He never abandons those who follow His commandments."

"Come travel with us again," they begged Rabbi Alfasi. But Rabbi Alfasi declined to go with them. When the people of Tunis had heard the amazing tale of his שבת in the desert, the prominent citizens of the Jewish community had approached Rabbi Alfasi and asked him to remain and be their leader. And there Rabbi Alfasi remained, leading the Tunisian Jewish community until his death in 1744.

Think & Share

What message do you think Hashem was sending R' Alfasi when He sent him the lion?

Expand Your Knowledge

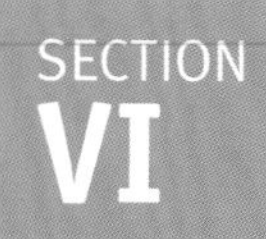

SECTION VI

THE ל"ט מלאכות

The following list of the thirty-nine אבות מלאכות follows the order of the Mishnah in שבת 73a. This list only provides definitions of the categories that are forbidden by Torah law (מִדְּאוֹרַיְתָא) and includes only a few of the תּוֹלָדוֹת. These thirty-nine labors were performed during the construction of the Mishkan. (Some authorities say that activities performed while offering קרבנות are also included.)

The first eleven אבות מלאכות are known as סִדּוּרָא דְפַת, the Order for Bread. All of these acts are needed in the process of baking bread. These were all performed in the Mishkan in the preparation of dyes made from herbs which were used to color various coverings and curtains, or they were performed in making flour for the Korban Minchah offerings.

1 זוֹרֵעַ ~ Sowing

Sowing means to plant seeds in the ground so that they will grow. All forms of planting (grafting, planting trees, etc.) are included in this *melachah*. Watering a plant is a *toladah* of this *melachah*.

2 חוֹרֵשׁ ~ Plowing

Plowing means to soften the ground to prepare it for planting. This includes any type of digging intended to soften the earth in order to sow or plant.

3 קוֹצֵר ~ Reaping

Reaping means to detach a fruit, vegetable, or plant from the ground using a utensil that is commonly used for that purpose. Ripping wheat out of the ground or picking fruits off a tree by hand are תּוֹלָדוֹת of this *melachah*.

מְעַמֵּר ~ Gathering 4

Gathering means to gather grain or other produce into a single pile. This applies only to items that grow and only in the place where they grew, such as gathering fruits under the tree from which they have fallen.

דָשׁ ~ Threshing 5

Threshing means to separate inedible material from the food to which it is naturally attached. The primary example of this is removing the husk (shell) from a kernel of wheat. Threshing is done by pounding the grain with a rod, or by having an animal trample it. Removing the husk by hand is a *toladah* of this *melachah*.

זוֹרֶה ~ Winnowing 6

Winnowing means to throw grain into the wind with a pitchfork so that the wind will blow away the chaff (husk) and leave the grain behind. Throwing the grain to the wind by hand or blowing away the chaff with one's mouth is a *toladah* of this *melachah*.

בּוֹרֵר ~ Selecting 7

Selecting means to sort a mixture of food and inedible material by picking out the inedible material by hand. For example, one may not pick out pebbles that are mixed together with kernels of wheat.

The rules regarding this *melachah* are very complex and can apply to all sorts of situations. For example, according to many authorities, the laws of בּוֹרֵר apply also to a mixture of two edible foods, when a person wants to eat one food but not the other. It is forbidden to pick out the food that one does not want to eat.

8 טוֹחֵן ~ Grinding

Grinding means to grind grain into flour. Cutting vegetables into tiny pieces, crushing spices in a mortar, or sawing wood to produce sawdust are all תּוֹלָדוֹת of טוֹחֵן.

9 מְרַקֵּד ~ Sifting

Sifting means to separate inedible material from food by using a sieve or any other utensil designed for this purpose. An example of מְרַקֵּד is sifting flour to remove impurities before baking.

The אבות מלאכות of זוֹרֶה, בּוֹרֵר, and מְרַקֵּד share an important characteristic: separating desired items from undesired items. The differences between them are discussed in the Gemara and its commentators.

10 לָשׁ ~ Kneading

Kneading means to mix together a liquid and a solid, such as flour and water, to form a dough.

11 אוֹפֶה ~ Baking

This *melachah* actually includes both baking and cooking. In fact, it is derived from the cooking of herbs in the making of dyes for the Mishkan.

This completes the מלאכות of סִדּוּרָא דְפַת. The next thirteen מלאכות are activities necessary for the production of wool. Wool was used for the covering and curtains in the Mishkan. The wool was obtained by shearing sheep.

12 גּוֹזֵז ~ Shearing

Shearing means to cut the wool or hair off an animal, whether it is alive or dead. It also includes cutting wool or hair from an animal hide. Cutting human hair or nails is a *toladah* of this *melachah*.

מְלַבֵּן ~ Whitening 13

Whitening is done by washing wool or flax to remove impurities. Some authorities are of the opinion that washing clothing is a *toladah* of this *melachah*, while others consider this part of the *av melachah*.

מְנַפֵּץ ~ Disentangling 14

Disentangling means to untangle clumps of wool by separating the individual fibers by hand. This is done before raw wool can be spun into thread. According to another opinion, מְנַפֵּץ means beating raw wool with sticks to remove sand and dirt.

צוֹבֵעַ ~ Dyeing 15

Dyeing is to permanently color an item as was done in the Mishkan when the wool was dyed for the colorful tapestries used as coverings and curtains.

טוֹוֶה ~ Spinning 16

Spinning means to twist together individual fibers of raw wool to form thread. This *melachah* is mentioned specifically in the Torah regarding the construction of the Mishkan (שמות 35:25-26).

מֵסֵךְ ~ Warping 17

Warping is the first step in the weaving process. This *melachah* consists of tying parallel threads from the front roller of a loom to its back roller. These threads are called the warp threads. Beating the threads to straighten them (called שׁוֹבֵט) is a *toladah* of warping.

18 עוֹשֶׂה שְׁנֵי בָּתֵּי נִירִין ~ Setting Two Heddles

Cloth is woven on a loom by weaving a thread (called a weft) over and under the warp threads. To weave, the weft thread is passed from side to side over and under the warp threads. In one direction, it crosses over every odd thread and under every even thread, and in the other direction it crosses over every even thread and under every odd thread. To make this easier to do, each warp thread is run through a ring that is fastened to one of two frames, the odd threads on one frame and the even threads on the other frame. When these frames are lifted, they lift the warp threads that are attached to them so that the weft thread can be passed through. Passing two warp threads through the rings of these frames is the *av melachah* of עוֹשֶׂה שְׁנֵי בָּתֵּי נִירִין.

19 אוֹרֵג שְׁנֵי חוּטִין ~ Weaving

Weaving is accomplished by passing the weft thread over and under the warp threads that are tied to the loom rollers. A person who passes the weft between the warp threads twice has violated the *melachah* of weaving.

20 פּוֹצֵעַ שְׁנֵי חוּטִין ~ Cutting Two Threads

Removing two threads means to remove two threads from the warp or weft of the woven material for a constructive purpose, such as to reweave a torn garment (*Rambam*). According to another opinion, it means to cut away a newly woven piece of cloth from the warp threads (*Raavad*).

21 קוֹשֵׁר ~ Knotting

Knotting means to tie a knot with the intent that it remain tied indefinitely. This *melachah* was performed in the Mishkan by weavers who would knot together warp threads that had snapped. This was also done by fishermen who knotted ropes to make nets for catching the *chilazon*, a sea creature whose blood was used in making the dye for תְּכֵלֶת (*blue wool*) for the Mishkan.

22 מַתִּיר ~ Untying

Untying means to untie a knot that was intended to remain as a permanent one. The fishermen who would catch the *chilazon* would sometimes untie old nets in order to reuse the rope in making new nets.

23 תּוֹפֵר שְׁתֵּי תְּפִירוֹת ~ Sewing Two Stitches

The *melachah* of sewing is performed by stitching together two pieces of cloth. As soon as a person sews a second stitch, he has violated this *melachah*. The covering of the Mishkan was made by sewing together cloth panels. The *toladah* of this *melachah* goes beyond sewing and includes any means by which two separate items are attached to one another. Gluing together papers or hides is a *toladah* of this *melachah*.

24 קוֹרֵעַ ~ Tearing

Tearing means to tear a cloth in order to resew it. For example, if a worm eats a hole in a cloth, it cannot be resewn properly unless the material is first torn so that the edges can be fit together to form a neat seam. This *melachah* was performed in the Mishkan when such holes were found in the cloth panels of the coverings.

This completes the thirteen מלאכות performed in the production of wool. The next six מלאכות (and, according to Rashi, #33 as well — see there) were performed in the Mishkan when dealing with the tachash, an animal whose hide was used for the coverings.

25 צָד ~ Trapping

Trapping means to capture an untamed creature (such as a deer) by grasping it with one's hands or forcing it into a small area where it can be easily captured. The creature must be difficult to capture, not sickly or slow-moving, or already confined to a small space. This *melachah* was used in the capturing of the *tachash*, whose hide was used for the coverings of the Mishkan. It was also used in the capture of the *chilazon* whose blood was used to make תְּכֵלֶת (*blue wool*).

26 שׁוֹחֵט ~ Slaughtering

Slaughtering means to kill any living creature by cutting its throat, stabbing it, or striking it a blow. Killing a creature by strangling it is a *toladah* of this *melachah*.

This *melachah* prohibits us from taking the life of any living creature on שבת, be it man, beast, fish, bird or insect.

27 מַפְשִׁיט ~ Skinning

Skinning means to remove the hide of a dead animal in order to make use of it.

28 מְעַבֵּד ~ Tanning (מוֹלֵחַ ~ Salting)

This *melachah* is performed by tanning or salting animal hides to prepare them for use.

The Mishnah in שבת (73a) lists Tanning and Salting as two separate מלאכות. However, the Gemara (75b) states that since salting is part of the tanning process, it should not be listed as a separate *av melachah*. Instead, the Gemara counts מְשַׂרְטֵט (Tracing Lines) as a *melachah* (#33).

29 מְמַחֵק ~ Scraping

Scraping means to smooth the animal hide by scraping off its hair.

30 מְחַתֵּךְ ~ Cutting

Cutting means to cut an animal hide to a specific size or shape.

31 כּוֹתֵב ~ Writing

This *melachah* is performed when a person writes any two letters, in any language, either two identical letters (אא) or two different letters (אב). Rambam is of the opinion that one is liable for writing the same letter twice only if the letters form a word (such as "תת" which means "give").

The act of writing was performed in the Mishkan by inscribing letters upon the beams that formed the walls of the Mishkan. This was done so that when the Mishkan was disassembled and reassembled, the beams would be replaced in their correct locations.

מוֹחֵק ~ Erasing 32

Erasing means to erase letters or markings in order to make a blank space to be able to write two letters or more.

מְשַׂרְטֵט ~ Tracing Lines 33

Before cutting leather, it was customary to trace lines on it, to mark the pattern on which the cuts were to be made. In the Mishkan, this was done before cutting the hides for the coverings. According to Rashi, this is the *av melachah* of tracing lines.

According to Rambam, מְשַׂרְטֵט is to scratch lines onto a parchment to help the *sofer* (scribe) write evenly.

בּוֹנֶה ~ Building 34

Building means to join together different things to form a unified whole, as is done when building a structure. Inserting the handle of an axe into its socket is a *toladah* of this *melachah*.

סוֹתֵר ~ Demolishing 35

Demolishing means to destroy a structure in order to build a new structure in its place. When demolishing does not serve a constructive purpose, it is not a violation of this *melachah* מִדְּאוֹרַיְתָא.

36 מְכַבֶּה ~ Extinguishing a Fire

This *av melachah* means to put out a flame or a glowing coal. All forms of extinguishing are prohibited either by the Torah (מִדְּאוֹרַיְתָא) or Rabbinically (מִדְּרַבָּנָן).

37 מַבְעִיר ~ Kindling a Fire

Kindling a fire is to kindle a fire for its heat or its light.

38 מַכֶּה בְּפַטִּישׁ ~ Finishing

מַכֶּה בְּפַטִּישׁ literally means striking (the final blow) with a hammer. This means to put the finishing touch on an object which is basically complete, for example: to tap lightly on a metal vessel to smooth it out or to tap on a brick to bring it in line with the others in its row.

39 מוֹצִיא מֵרְשׁוּת לִרְשׁוּת ~ Transferring from One Domain to Another

Transferring from one domain to another means to carry an object from a רְשׁוּת הַיָּחִיד (*private domain*) to a רְשׁוּת הָרַבִּים (*public domain*) and putting it down there. Carrying an object from a רְשׁוּת הָרַבִּים (*public domain*) to a רְשׁוּת הַיָּחִיד (*private domain*) is forbidden as well. However, there is a difference of opinion among the authorities whether this is part of the *av melachah* or it is a *toladah* of the *melachah*.

It is also forbidden to carry an object a distance of four אַמּוֹת in a רְשׁוּת הָרַבִּים (public domain). There is also a difference of opinion whether this is included in the *av melachah* or if it is a *toladah*.

Determine Mastery

REVIEWING KEY INFORMATION

1. What does Hashem want us to remember when we refrain from doing a melachah on שבת?
2. What are the five requirements necessary for a melachah to be considered a מְלֶאכֶת מַחְשֶׁבֶת?
3. What is an av melachah? What is a toladah?
4. What does שבת commemorate?
5. What do we mean when we say that the שבת is מֵעֵין עוֹלָם הַבָּא?

CRITICAL THINKING

1. How does our story about R' Alfasi illustrate the words of the zemer כִּי אֶשְׁמְרָה שַׁבָּת קֵל יִשְׁמְרֵנִי?

לע"נ ר' עקיבא בן ר' מאיר זאב ז"ל
לע"נ רחל בת ר' יוסף ז"ל
למשפחת לנסברג

Dave and Judy Landsberg
Effy and Tzivie Landsberg

מצוה

33

MITZVAH

Honor Your Father and Mother

מצוות כיבוד אב ואם

MITZVAH **33**

מצות כיבוד אב ואם

Honor Your Father and Mother

THE MITZVAH

A person must honor his father and mother and assist them with all their needs.

- כִּבּוּד
- הַכָּרַת הַטּוֹב
- יִרְאַת אָב וָאֵם
- בְּסֵבֶר פָּנִים יָפוֹת
- עַנְיֵי הַכָּבוֹד
- שֻׁתָּפִין
- קֶרֶן
- יַאֲרִכוּן

SECTION I

Introduction to the Mitzvah

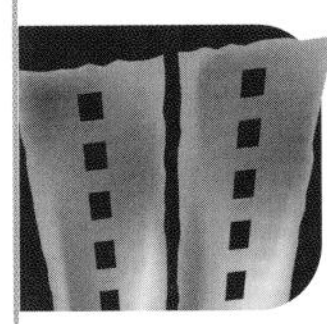

It was almost twenty-four hours since the elderly man had been brought to the hospital emergency room. During that entire time, the man's son had not left his father's bedside, to ensure that his father was given the best possible care throughout his stay.

The elderly man looked up from his bed and said to his son, "You are so devoted to me! What did I ever do to deserve such a good son?" His son replied, "Father, whatever I am doing for you now is nothing compared to what you and mother have done for me since the day I was born."

Our parents do so much for us; they bring us into this world, clothe us, feed us, educate us, and provide for all our needs. They are always looking out for what is best for us. How much gratitude and הַכָּרַת הַטּוֹב must we have for our parents, the people who brought us into being and worked hard to raise us?

The mitzvah of honoring parents is, according to many authorities, based on a person's obligation to express הַכָּרַת הַטּוֹב to his parents.

Showing הַכָּרַת הַטּוֹב to our parents also makes us aware of all the good that our Father in Heaven, Hashem, does for us. He instilled in each of us a נשמה, provides all our needs, and watches over us every moment of every day. If the Torah obligates us to honor parents, how much more so should we honor Hashem? We do this by faithfully observing the מצוות He gave us.

~ Sefer HaChinuch §33

Why do children have to honor their parents even if they do not provide for their children's needs?

The Source of the Mitzvah

SECTION II

כַּבֵּד אֶת אָבִיךָ וְאֶת אִמֶּךָ

שמות כ:יב פרשת יתרו

Honor your father and your mother

In this mitzvah, the Torah mentions the father before the mother. However, in פרשת קדושים (ויקרא 19:3), when the Torah commands us to hold our parents in awe (Mitzvah 212, יראת אב ואם), it mentions the mother before the father, as the פסוק states, אִישׁ אִמּוֹ וְאָבִיו תִּירָאוּ.

The Gemara (*Kiddushin* 30b-31a) explains that a child is likely to honor his mother more than his father, because his mother speaks to him with gentle words, coaxing him to do things for her. Therefore, the Torah mentions the father first, to teach us that a child should honor his father and his mother equally.

In the mitzvah to hold one's parents in awe, the Torah mentions the mother first because a child is likely to revere his father more, since his father is the one who teaches him Torah. (In earlier generations, a father was often his child's main teacher.) Therefore, the Torah mentions the mother first in that mitzvah, to teach us that they should be equally held in awe.

~ *Rambam*, הלכות ממרים 6:2

Did You Know?

Even actions that have no direct connection to one's parents can bring them honor. Therefore, a person who truly wishes to bring honor to his parents should study Torah and perform מצוות, as this is the greatest way to honor them.

~ *Kitzur Shulchan Aruch* §143:21

Reading Check

Why does the Torah state "Honor your father and your mother," and not "Honor your mother and your father?"

A person must honor his father and mother and assist them with all their needs.

SECTION III

The Laws of the Mitzvah

1. A person must honor his parents both in his speech and in his actions.

2. A person must serve his parents and help them with any of their needs, such as food, drink, and clothing. He must do this pleasantly (בְּסֵבֶר פָּנִים יָפוֹת), to show that honoring his parents is not a burden, but something he is happy to do.

3. A child does not have to spend his own money to provide for his parents' needs, unless his parents do not have the money to do so themselves.

4. A person must stand up (קִימָה) when his parent comes into view. One must rise to his full height as soon as the parent comes into view, and may not sit down until the parent either disappears from view or sits down. A parent may forgo this honor. However, it is still a mitzvah for the child to show token honor by rising slightly from his seat, as if he intended to stand up.

5. A person may not violate a Torah law (מִדְּאוֹרַיְתָא) or a Rabbinic law (מִדְּרַבָּנָן) if his parent asks him to do so.

6. Although parents may forgo the honor due them — for example, by telling a child not to stand up for them (see Law 4) — parents may not allow their child to cause them pain or embarrassment, or permit their child to curse or hit them.

7. A person must honor his parents even after their death. It is customary for a son to recite *kaddish* and to lead the congregation in prayer as the *chazzan*, during the first eleven months following a parent's passing, and on the anniversary of a parent's death (*yahrzeit*). It is also customary to study Torah (particularly Mishnah) and give צדקה in their memory. In these ways, a person fulfills the mitzvah of honoring his parents even after their passing.

8. This mitzvah includes honoring other relatives as well. There are different opinions as to which relatives are included and which are מִדְּאוֹרַיְתָא and which are מִדְּרַבָּנָן. This list includes stepparents, older brothers, grandparents, in-laws, and parents' siblings.

9. This mitzvah applies to both men and women, in all places and at all times.

10. The reward for fulfilling this mitzvah is long life.

טוב טעם
Appreciating the Mitzvah

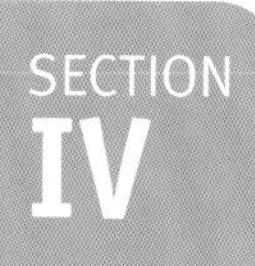

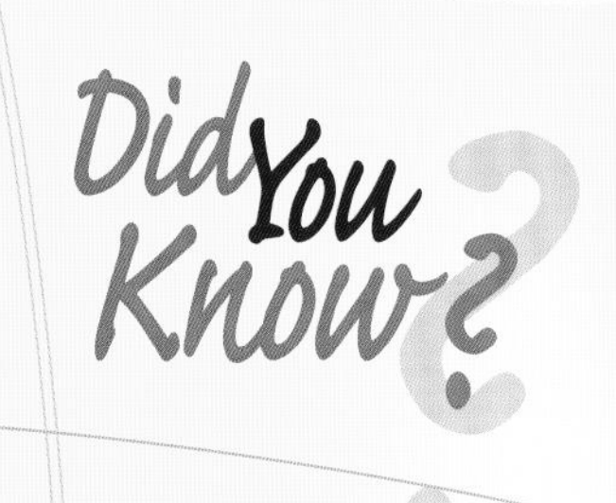

When the Jews were in the Midbar, little effort was needed to provide for one's children. מָן fell from the sky each day, water was always available from the באר of Miriam, and the עֲנְנֵי הַכָּבוֹד would launder their clothes. Yet, despite all this, Hashem commanded Bnei Yisrael, even those children in the Midbar, to honor their parents. From this we learn that a child must honor even a parent who did not provide for his needs.

~ *Meshech Chochmah*, דברים 5:16

The Key to the *Mesorah*

The king was a kind and generous leader. He had taken his subjects out of slavery, from under the rule of an evil, ruthless tyrant. It was no wonder that the king's subjects were so loyal to him and obeyed his every command.

But how would the next generation, and all those who would come after, know of all the great things the king had done for them? Born into a happy, successful, and peaceful society, they might take their good life for granted, and would not feel any loyalty toward the king. What would ensure that they would serve him loyally and obey his laws?

The only way to ensure that future generations know what has happened in the past, is for each new generation to look to their elders for guidance, and accept their teachings. The parents would teach their children of their king's greatness and kindness, and that all his commands must be carefully followed.

Hashem took us out of מצרים and freed us from slavery. He took us to הר סיני and gave us the Torah. He made us His special nation. These are historical facts that we know to be true, because the truth of these events has been faithfully transmitted from parent to child; every child hears them from his parents, and accepts them as true.

The foundations of our faith have survived through the ages because of the respect children have for their parents. In this way, honoring one's parents ensures the continuity of the Jewish nation. We learn from our parents about the existence of Hashem, the Jewish way of life, our history, and the teachings of the Torah. And just as we look to our parents, so too, one day, our children will look to us.

~ Sefer HaIkkarim and Rabbi Samson Raphael Hirsch, Commentary to שמות *20:12*

A person must honor his father and mother and assist them with all their needs.

Partners with Hashem

There are three שֻׁתָּפִין, *partners,* in the making of a person: Hashem, the father, and the mother. Therefore, just as Hashem commands us to honor Him, so too, He commands us to honor His partners in our creation.

When a person honors his father and mother, Hashem says, "I consider it as if I was living there with them, and he honored Me as well."

~ *Kiddushin* 30b

Reward for Fulfilling the Mitzvah

This is one of only two מצוות where the Torah tells us the reward for its fulfillment. The Torah tells us (שמות 20:12), לְמַעַן יַאֲרִכוּן יָמֶיךָ, *so that your days will be lengthened.* One who fulfills this mitzvah will enjoy long life.

The Mishnah tells us that for some מצוות, the reward a person receives in this world is only the פֵּרוֹת, the *fruits* of the mitzvah, while the קֶרֶן, the *principal*, remains untouched for him to enjoy in the next world. Honoring one's parents is one such mitzvah. A person who honors his parents will enjoy long life in this world, and enjoy a complete reward in עולם הבא as well.

~ *Pe'ah* 1:1

This mitzvah is cherished by Hashem so much that He greatly rewards those who are careful in performing it. Even Eisav, who committed many sins, was richly rewarded for his excellence in כִּבּוּד אָב וָאֵם. He took extreme care in honoring his father, Yitzchak, and was granted Rome and its powerful empire because of this mitzvah. If Hashem repaid a רשע to such an extent, how much more so will He reward a person who honors his parents and performs other מצוות as well!

~ see *Tanchuma, Kedoshim* §15

The first of the לוחות contains מצוות that are between man and Hashem, while the second לוח contains מצוות that are between man and his fellow man. Why is כִּבּוּד אָב וָאֵם listed on the first לוח?

MITZVAH 25
MITZVAH 26
MITZVAH 27
MITZVAH 28
MITZVAH 29
MITZVAH 30
MITZVAH 31
MITZVAH 32
MITZVAH 33
MITZVAH 34
MITZVAH 35
MITZVAH 36
MITZVAH 37
MITZVAH 38

Living the Mitzvah

Dama ben Nesinah

In the time of the second בית המקדש, there was a Roman by the name of Dama ben Nesinah who lived in Ashkelon. He was an important official in the region, and socialized with the Roman aristocracy. He was a very important man, yet he always showed his parents honor and respect. He never felt that it was beneath him.

Once, his mother (who was mentally ill) slapped him in the presence of his fellow dignitaries. As she did so, she dropped her glove. Dama immediately picked up the glove and handed it back to her, so she would not suffer any distress.

Another time, Dama was seated among the aristocrats of Rome, dressed in a gold-embroidered silk cloak. His mother stepped up to him and ripped off his cloak, hit him on the head, and spat in his face. Yet Dama did nothing to embarrass her!

In fact, the Gemara (Kiddushin 31a) uses Dama ben Nesinah as a prime example of someone who properly honored his parents.

R' Eliezer's students asked him, "To what extent must a person honor his parents?"

He answered them, "Go and see how a certain non-Jew, Dama ben Nesinah, behaved toward his father." The incident to which R' Eliezer referred is illustrated by the following story:

A person must honor his father and mother and assist them with all their needs.

The אֵפוֹד, one of the eight garments that the Kohen Gadol wore, had two stones, the אַבְנֵי שֹׁהַם, set upon its shoulder-straps. It happened that these stones, which were extremely rare, needed to be replaced. The חכמים heard that Dama ben Nesinah had such stones, so they traveled to Ashkelon to pay him a visit.

Dama ben Nesinah received the Jewish leaders with deference. He did indeed have the stones they needed for sale, and would gladly do business with them. They negotiated for a while, and agreed on a price. Dama would make a profit of six hundred thousand gold *dinars* from the sale of his gems!

After the deal was struck, Dama went to get the stones. He kept them in a locked box, and had to get the key. He told the חכמים that he would be back very soon with the stones.

Almost immediately, however, Dama was back, and without the precious gems! He apologized to the חכמים, and told them that he could not complete the transaction at this time.

"The key to the box where I keep the gems is under my father's pillow," explained Dama. "He is asleep right now, and I will not wake him."

The חכמים could not wait, and went elsewhere to buy the stones. Dama lost the opportunity to sell the stones and earn that huge profit.

Hashem, however, saw the honor that Dama ben Nesinah had given his father. Dama would not disturb his father's sleep, even though he would lose an enormous profit. Hashem repaid Dama ben Nesinah for the respect he showed his father. The next year, a פָּרָה אֲדֻמָּה, a "*red cow,*" was born in Dama's herd.

A פָּרָה אֲדֻמָּה is very rare. Its ashes are used to make the מי חטאת, a special mixture that is sprinkled on a person who became טמא by coming in contact with a dead person. The ashes of the פָּרָה אֲדֻמָּה are needed to purify the person and make him טהור again.

A person must honor his father and mother and assist them with all their needs.

The חכמים visited Dama ben Nesinah again, this time to purchase the פָּרָה אֲדֻמָּה. Dama said to them, "I know that even if I asked you for all the money in the world for this cow, you would give it to me. However, I will ask you only for the amount of money I forfeited on account of my father's honor."

The חכמים agreed and the deal was done. Bnei Yisrael had a פָּרָה אֲדֻמָּה, and Dama ben Nesinah received his money. Hashem had rewarded Dama ben Nesinah and repaid what he had given up.

R' Chanina commented on Dama's reward: If one who performs a mitzvah that he was not commanded to do receives such a rich reward, how much more will a person who *was* commanded to do the mitzvah receive as a reward when he fulfills it! For R' Chanina would always say: גָּדוֹל הַמְּצֻוֶּה וְעוֹשֶׂה מִמִּי שֶׁאֵינוֹ מְצֻוֶּה וְעוֹשֶׂה, *Greater is the person who is commanded to do a mitzvah and does it than one who is not commanded to do it and does it.*

Which Mishnah in פרקי אבות is illustrated by the fact that we can learn how to properly perform כִּבּוּד אָב וָאֵם from Dama ben Nesinah?

Expand Your Knowledge

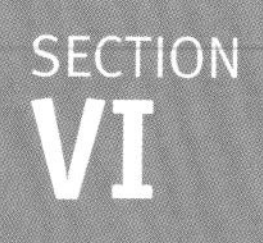

SECTION VI

The Blessing for the Mitzvah:

There are many מצוות *which we perform without reciting a berachah.* כִּבּוּד אָב וָאֵם *is such a mitzvah. Below are several reasons why we do not recite a berachah when we perform this mitzvah:*

1 *This is a mitzvah that is dependent upon the wishes and acceptance of another person* — A person does not recite a *berachah* when visiting the sick or when giving *tzedakah*, since the sick person may not want to see the visitor at that particular moment, and the poor person may refuse to accept the charity. So too, a person does not recite a *berachah* upon this mitzvah, since the parent may want to decline the honor being given him.

~ see תשובות הרשב"א I:18

2 *This is a mitzvah which applies at all times* — Generally, a *berachah* is recited only on מצוות that have to be fulfilled at a specific time, such as ציצית and *succah*.

~ see *Ohr Zarua* I:40

3 *This is a mitzvah between man and his fellow man* — Just as there is no *berachah* when a person performs other מצוות that are בין אדם לחבירו, such as acts of *chessed* and *tzedakah*, there is no *berachah* for performing this mitzvah.

~ *Kessef Mishneh* to *Rambam*, הלכות ברכות 11:2

Determine Mastery

REVIEWING KEY INFORMATION

1. Which important middah is at the root of this mitzvah?
2. Why does the Torah mention the father first in this mitzvah, while, in the mitzvah commanding us to hold our parents in awe, it mentions the mother first?
3. What is the halachah regarding standing up for a parent?
4. When is a person obligated to refuse his parents' requests?
5. Why is this mitzvah so important to our mesorah?
6. Explain the term מצווה ועושה, and what you learned about it.
7. Give at least two reasons why we do not make a berachah on this mitzvah.

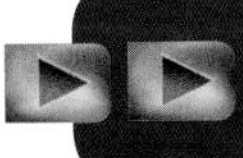

CRITICAL THINKING

1. How should fulfilling this mitzvah affect the way we serve Hashem?

INVESTIGATE AND INQUIRE

1. Throughout Tanach, there are examples of כִּבּוּד אָב וָאֵם. List as many as you can.

לעילוי נשמת

אליהו צבי בן ר׳ יוסף שמעון נ״י

Dedicated by

Jerry and Esther Williams

מצוה

MITZVAH 34

Do Not Murder

איסור רציחה

MITZVAH **34**

איסור רציחה

Do Not Murder

THE MITZVAH

It is forbidden to murder a person, or to cause his death indirectly.

- רְצִיחָה
- מְחַלֵּל
- עָרֵי מִקְלָט
- אִנָּה
- חָבִיב
- צֶלֶם אֱלֹקִים
- גּוֹאֲלֵי הַדָּם

SECTION I Introduction to the Mitzvah

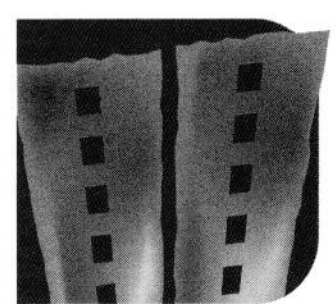
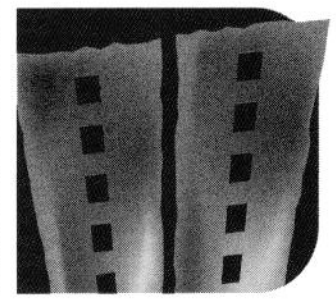

Can we put a price on human life? Life is so precious that the Torah commands us to be מְחַלֵּל שַׁבָּת if it will prolong a person's life even by a minute or two. Each moment of a person's life is an opportunity to serve Hashem, and we must not give away even a second of that time.

Just as there is nothing more precious than a moment of human life, there is nothing more destructive than taking a human life. Once a life is lost, it can never be replaced. Even if a murderer regrets his action and does תְּשׁוּבָה, he can never fully erase his evil deed, for by murdering his victim, he has also destroyed all future generations that would have descended from the murdered person.

~ see Mishnah, *Sanhedrin* 37a

Rambam writes: The act of רְצִיחָה, *murder*, is more destructive to the world than any other *aveirah*. The Rambam adds that anyone guilty of this crime is a רָשָׁע גָּמוּר, *an absolute rasha*, and all the מצוות he performs in his lifetime cannot offset this *aveirah* and save him from being punished.

~ *Rambam*, הלכות רוצח 4:9

The murder of another person deprives Hashem of one of His servants. Although Hashem has many servants who carry out His will, the absence of even a single person is significant. Every person has a specific role in the service of Hashem that cannot be filled by any other person.

~ ליקוטי הלכות, *Pesach* 28:9

After Kayin killed Hevel, Hashem told him, קוֹל דְּמֵי אָחִיךָ צוֹעֲקִים אֵלַי מִן הָאֲדָמָה, Your brother's "bloods" cry out to Me from the earth. Why did Hashem use the plural word דְּמֵי, "bloods," rather than דָּם, "blood"?

The Source of the Mitzvah

SECTION II

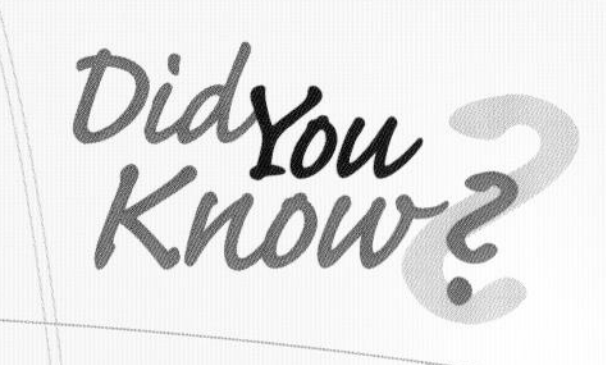

A man mints many coins from one mold, and they are all alike. However, Hashem created all mankind from the mold of אדם הראשון, meaning that every person is descended from אדם, yet no two people are alike.

~ see *Mishnah, Sanhedrin* 37a

לֹא תִרְצָח

שמות כ:יג פרשת יתרו

Do not murder

The עשרת הדברות are divided into two groups: The first לוח contains the five מצוות that are בין אדם למקום, between a person and Hashem; on the second לוח are the remaining five מצוות that are בין אדם לחבירו, between a person and his fellow man.

The prohibition against רְצִיחָה was placed directly opposite the first commandment at the head of the first לוח, אָנֹכִי ה׳. This is to teach us that just as denying Hashem's existence is the worst *aveirah* one can commit against Hashem, רְצִיחָה is the worst *aveirah* a person can commit against his fellow man.

~ עקידת יצחק §45

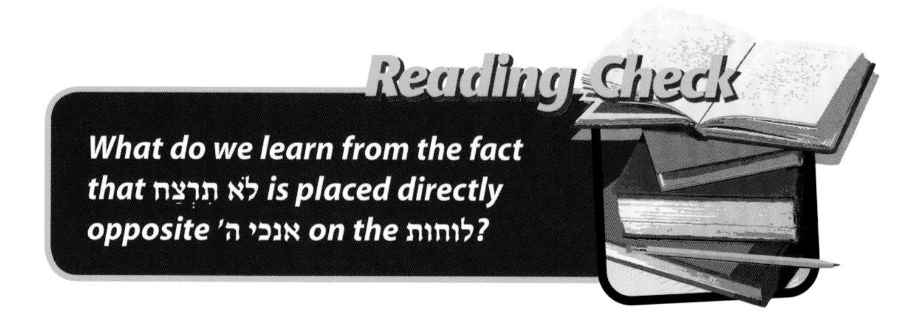

What do we learn from the fact that לֹא תִרְצָח is placed directly opposite אנכי ה׳ on the לוחות?

It is forbidden to murder a person, or to cause his death indirectly.

SECTION III The Laws of the Mitzvah

1. It is forbidden to murder any person — man or woman, adult or child. It is also forbidden to cause a person's death indirectly. This includes hiring someone else to murder the person. It also includes an action such as tying the person up and putting him in front of a lion so that the lion will kill him.

2. It is also forbidden to do anything that will cause a terminally ill or dying person to die more quickly.

3. A murderer receives the death penalty only if he intended to kill (בְּמֵזִיד), and only if he killed the person he wanted to kill, and not a different person. The penalty for murder is execution by beheading (הֶרֶג), if the murderer was properly warned (הַתְרָאָה) and there were two valid witnesses who saw the murder.

4. A person violates this prohibition but does not receive the death penalty if he murdered a *tereifah*, a person with one of certain specific physical defects that will certainly cause him to die.

5. A person who kills unintentionally (בְּשׁוֹגֵג) violates this prohibition, but does not receive the death penalty. Rather, he is exiled to one of the עָרֵי מִקְלָט, *cities of refuge* [see Mitzvah 408, Mitzvah 410, and Mitzvah 520].

6. This prohibition applies to both men and women, in all places and at all times. As a general rule, all of the Torah's prohibitions (מצוות לא תעשה) apply equally to men and women. Non-Jews are also forbidden to murder, as a prohibition against murder is one of the שֶׁבַע מִצְוֹת בְּנֵי נֹחַ.

7. A person must sacrifice his life rather than commit murder or hand someone over to be killed. This is one of the three מצוות that a Jew must not violate, even if it means giving up his life (יֵהָרֵג וְאַל יַעֲבוֹר).

טוב טעם
Appreciating the Mitzvah

SECTION IV

Murder Terminates the Victim's Potential

Hashem gave us each a נשמה. Our purpose in this world is to perfect and uplift that נשמה. We must constantly strive to reach higher levels of *kedushah* by learning Torah, performing מצוות, and refraining from doing עבירות. Every mitzvah a person does elevates his נשמה to a higher level.

When a murderer takes a life, he severs the נשמה of the victim from his body. The victim can no longer perfect his נשמה and fulfill the task Hashem gave him in this world. The murderer has therefore robbed his victim of his life's true purpose.

~ *R' Saadiah Gaon,* אמונות ודעות 3:2

Murder Minimizes the Glory of Hashem

The Jewish people have been given the mission of spreading Hashem's glory in this world. We accomplish this by demonstrating to all mankind the greatness of the nation that received the Torah and lives by its God-given teachings. The Navi makes this point when he states (*Yeshayah* 43:21): עַם זוּ יָצַרְתִּי לִי תְּהִלָּתִי יְסַפֵּרוּ, *This people I formed for My sake; they will relate My praise.*

A murderer deprives the world of an "ambassador" of Hashem and His Torah, thereby lessening Hashem's glory.

~ *Derech Pikudecha,* לא תעשה §34, *Cheilek HaMachshavah* §2

By commanding us not to kill, Hashem is warning us not to destroy that which He made for His honor, for each person is created to bring glory to Hashem and to give thanks to Him.

~ *Ramban,* שמות 20:13

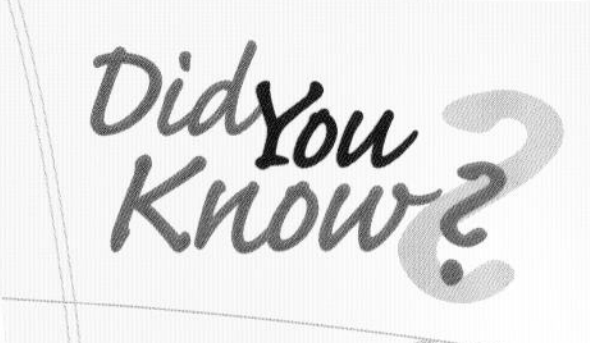

If a group of Jews is threatened with death unless they hand over a member of their group to be killed, they must all sacrifice their lives rather than hand over a single person to be killed.

~ *Rambam,* הלכות יסודי התורה 5:5

It is forbidden to murder a person, or to cause his death indirectly.

☙ The Murderer Attacks Hashem's Image

Rabbi Akiva (אבות 3:18) says, חָבִיב אָדָם שֶׁנִּבְרָא בְּצֶלֶם, *Beloved (by Hashem) is man, for he was created* בְּצֶלֶם אֱלֹקִים, *in Hashem's image*. Therefore, in addition to killing a servant of God, the act of murder is a direct insult to Hashem's honor. Man was created in the image of his Creator. To attack a human being is to attack a likeness of Hashem.

This is why embarrassing someone in public is like murdering him. When someone is embarrassed, the blood drains from his face — the face that bears the reflection of Hashem. A person who causes this to happen has "damaged" the Divine Image.

~ *Alshich*, בראשית 9:6

One Who Saves a Life

Chazal tell us that a person who murders is considered as if he destroyed an entire world. This is to teach us and reinforce within us that the potential and worth of each person is so great that destroying even a single person is devastating. Chazal go on to tell us that for this very same reason, whoever preserves a single life is considered as if he has saved a whole world.

~ see Mishnah, *Sanhedrin* 37a

What acts can we do that would be considered "saving a life" other than physically saving a person from harm?

Living the Mitzvah

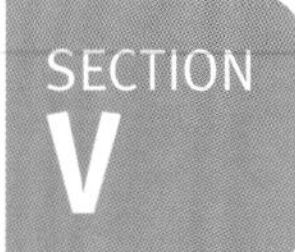

SECTION V

There Is No Escaping Hashem

*The Torah makes it very clear that a person is not allowed to murder. This offense is punishable by death. In a secular criminal court, there are varying degrees of murder that, when judged in a court of law, will result in varying sentences of punishment. However, the Jewish judicial courts deal mainly with two types of murder: intentional and accidental. If a man struck another man, either with his hand or with a weapon, and meant to kill him, and at least two valid witnesses warned him beforehand of the penalty for his action (*הַתְרָאָה*) and then testified to the act, then the man is convicted by* בית דין *and sentenced to death by beheading.*

If a man killed someone accidentally in front of witnesses, then he must run to an עִיר מִקְלָט *(one of several special cities of refuge in Eretz Yisrael) and remain there until the death of the Kohen Gadol. This is a punishment for the murderer, for he must stay in exile, away from his family, his home, his livelihood, and all that is familiar to him. This is also a protection for him, as the victim's relatives (the* גּוֹאֲלֵי הַדָּם*) are allowed to pursue and kill their relative's murderer, unless he remains inside an* עִיר מִקְלָט *(see Mitzvah 410).*

As stated above, these things happen to the murderer (accidental or intentional) if there are witnesses. But what if there are no witnesses to the crime? Do such murderers go unpunished? Of course not! Hashem runs the world and He makes sure that justice is served. As the פסוק *(*שמות *21:13) states:* וְהָאֱלֹקִים אִנָּה לְיָדוֹ*, And God brought it about to his hand. Hashem arranges matters so that each man receives the punishment he deserves, as the following story illustrates.*

It is forbidden to murder a person, or to cause his death indirectly.

I

Hurmiz bar Nakim was not a nice man. Perhaps he once was, but circumstances which no one — not even Hurmiz himself — remembers, brought him to his current situation. Hurmiz was a highwayman who would ambush carriages that came down the road, and steal all the passengers' money and possessions. And Heaven help anyone who refused to give Hurmiz what he wanted! He would wait in the forest for an unsuspecting carriage to roll by on the adjacent road. If the carriage looked like it belonged to a wealthy individual, Hurmiz would make sure the owner felt obligated to share his wealth. If the carriage looked like it belonged to a poor person, Hurmiz would usually let it pass; not because he was a goodhearted person in any way, but because it was just not worth his time.

One late winter afternoon, as the sun was setting, Hurmiz waited in the forest. He had been waiting all day. The cold was seeping into his bones, but he would not budge. He had heard rumors of a very wealthy landowner who was traveling in the area, collecting rent from his various tenants. Hurmiz was looking forward to striking it rich. As the sky darkened, he heard the rumble of carriage wheels.

"That must be him now," thought Hurmiz. He readied himself to attack the carriage at the best possible spot. As the carriage rounded the bend, Hurmiz jumped out of his hiding place. The driver took one look at the fierce highwayman whose face was covered with a black cloth, and turned tail and ran. Hurmiz laughed. He let the driver go. All he wanted was the money inside the carriage.

The landowner, however, would not give up without a fight. If only he had been as smart as the cowardly driver. The rich man and Hurmiz scuffled, and Hurmiz, who had waited for this prize all day and was not leaving without it, finally dealt the man a vicious blow and killed him. Hurmiz took all the money, and anything else of value that he could find, and ran off into the night. No one saw him commit this atrocious crime; no one, that is, but the One Above.

II

Chaim, the peddler, had had a most successful day at the market, and a very good evening at the local inn as well. He had made a nice amount of money, and topped it off with good food and drink. Though the hour was getting late, he had promised his wife that he would be home that night, so he set off. He was traveling light and he spurred the horses to go as fast as they could. It was cold, and he wanted to get home. The horses were going so fast that Chaim did not see the large ditch in the road until it was too late. As the wagon hit the ditch, one of the wheels was knocked loose and the wagon tilted dangerously to one side.

Fortunately, Chaim was an experienced driver and did not panic. He slowed the horses and cautiously came to a stop. He stepped down from the wagon to survey the damage; he then got out his hammer and some nails and set to work. He was fortunate that the moon was shining brightly, so that he was able to see what he was doing. Chaim was so involved in his work that he swung his hammer too hard. As his arm swung down, the top of the hammer separated from the handle and went flying. He looked up to see where it had gone, and to his horror, saw that it had struck and killed a man.

The man, the rich man's driver, had been running from Hurmiz as if his life depended upon it, and did not see the hammer head coming straight at his head until it was much too late. Chaim saw that there was nothing that could be done for the poor man. Feeling very scared and not knowing what to do, Chaim quietly took up the reins and drove his wagon home. He never mentioned the incident to anyone. But of course the One Above knew all about it.

III

Hurmiz had had enough. With his ill-gotten gains, he could now afford posh accommodations. Yet, he had stayed in the forest these last few weeks, until the furor over the murder of the landowner had died down. But now he wanted a warm bed and a hot meal. He decided to go to the inn in town and spend the night in comfort. After all, he was a rich man now. Why shouldn't he enjoy his wealth, no matter how ill-gotten it was? He went to the inn, rented a room, and then ordered a hot meal. The inn was very crowded. He had forgotten that this was market day, and that all the peddlers and shopkeepers came here to eat and unwind after a hectic day. He couldn't find an empty seat. Finally, he spotted a seat in the corner, next to a ladder. He quickly took his food there and sat down.

Chaim, too, had been avoiding that infamous road these last few weeks. But business was business, and he needed to go back to town to peddle his wares...

It is forbidden to murder a person, or to cause his death indirectly.

Again, Chaim had a very successful day in town and went to the inn to celebrate. He got his food, but he too couldn't find a seat. Finally, he spotted the ladder in the corner, leaning against a narrow ledge. He could climb the ladder, perch on the ledge, and sit pretty comfortably. Chaim took his meal, climbed up the ladder, and made himself comfortable.

Just as Chaim was about to start eating, he remembered that he had left his drink at the counter. As Chaim started down the ladder, he lost his footing. Chaim toppled off the ladder, and landed right on top of Hurmiz, killing him. The inn was full of witnesses who testified that it had been an unfortunate accident. Chaim had to go into גלות, to an עיר מקלט, and Hurmiz received the punishment he deserved for intentionally killing an innocent man. There is no escaping Hashem, the true Judge.

Which of the י״ג עִקָּרִים, the Rambam's 13 Principles of Faith, are demonstrated in this story?

Expand Your Knowledge

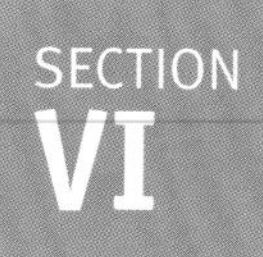

ארבע מיתות בית דין

In the times when the בית המקדש stood and the Great Sanhedrin convened there, any בית דין of twenty-three judges (called a lesser Sanhedrin) could decide both civil (monetary) and criminal cases (see *Rambam,* הלכות סנהדרין 14:11-14). When someone committed a crime for which the punishment was death, there were four types of executions that בית דין could carry out.

Of course, בית דין would only sentence a person to death after making absolutely certain that the person had been warned by two valid witnesses before he committed his crime that he would be punished by death (הַתְרָאָה). Also, two valid witnesses had to testify in בית דין that they saw him actually commit the crime.

A בית דין must be certain that a person is guilty before it carries out the death penalty. In fact, the Gemara (מכות 7a) states that according to one opinion, a Sanhedrin who executed even one person in seventy years was known as a "destroyer" Sanhedrin.

The אַרְבַּע מִיתוֹת בֵּית דִּין (the four types of executions) are:

סְקִילָה — *stoning*
שְׂרֵיפָה — *burning*
הֶרֶג — *beheading*
חֶנֶק — *strangling*

Determine Mastery

REVIEWING KEY INFORMATION

1. Why is no sin as destructive as the sin of murder?
2. What is the punishment for a person who murdered במזיד, with התראה and עדים?
3. What is the punishment for unintentional murder?
4. When is a Jew obligated to let himself be killed?
5. Why is murder an assault on the victim's נשמה as well as his body?
6. Where does the Torah teach us that no one can escape Hashem's judgment? Explain.

CRITICAL THINKING

1. What can we learn from the fact that Hashem created אדם הראשון, alone, and no one else at the same time?

INVESTGATE AND INQUIRE

1. Who was the first murderer mentioned in the Torah, and what was his eventual fate?

מוקדש לזכות
כל היחידים בכלל ישראל
הזקוקים לשידוך הגון בעיתו

מ צ ו ה

35

MITZVAH

Do Not Commit Adultery

איסור אשת איש

MITZVAH **35**

איסור אשת איש

Do Not Commit Adultery

THE MITZVAH

A marriage-type relationship between a man and another man's wife is forbidden.

- טֻמְאָה
- אֵירוּסִין
- נִשּׂוּאִין
- אֵשֶׁת אִישׁ
- מֵי הַמָּרִים
- עַיִן רוֹאָה
- אֹזֶן שׁוֹמַעַת
- שְׁלוֹם בַּיִת
- גֵט

SECTION I

Introduction to the Mitzvah

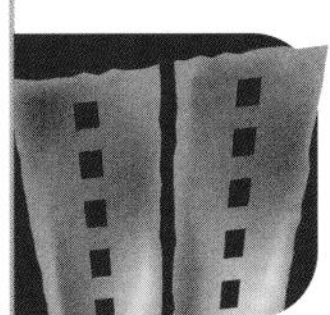

The Jewish people have always known the importance of family. One of the foundations of our faith and our society is the continuation of our *mesorah*, which is transmitted from parent to child.

Can you imagine a world where families did not exist? Can you imagine a world where children did not know who their parents or siblings were; a world where fathers did not know their own children?

In a world like that, fathers would not be able to teach their children; nor could they ensure that their children follow in the ways of the Torah, for they would not know who their children were! In fact, a world like that would resemble Mitzrayim, which was so full of immorality that the Egyptians were on the lowest level of טֻמְאָה, *impurity*.

The Jewish nation was redeemed from Mitzrayim because they did not fall prey to the טֻמְאָה of the Egyptians. They kept themselves separate, and kept their family units intact. They kept the *kedushah* of the Jewish family alive.

The bond of marriage brings that *kedushah* into the Jewish home, and ensures our survival as a מַמְלֶכֶת כֹּהֲנִים and a גּוֹי קָדוֹשׁ.

Hashem designated a wife for each man, an עֵזֶר כְּנֶגְדּוֹ. Every unique person has been given an equally unique spouse so that together they can serve Hashem and build a family.

When a married woman and a man who is not her husband commit the terrible sin of לֹא תִנְאָף, they break the bond between husband and wife, and the special *kedushah* of marriage is lost.

Think & Share

In a world where the family unit did not exist, why would observing the מצוות be difficult?

The Source of the Mitzvah

SECTION II

לֹא תִנְאָף

שמות כ:יג פרשת יתרו

Do not commit adultery

One might have thought that this prohibition applies to all types of forbidden relationships. However, the Torah always uses the term ניאוף to refer specifically to the sin of adultery — a forbidden relationship between a married woman and a man other than her husband (see, for example, ויקרא 20:10). Therefore, it is clear that the prohibition of לֹא תִנְאָף applies only to a forbidden relationship with a married woman.

~ *Rashi* to שמות 20:13

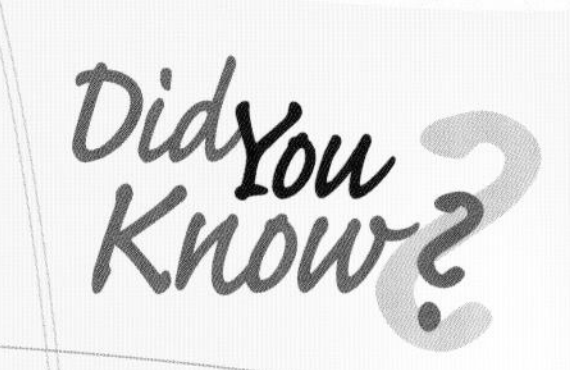

אֵירוּסִין (kiddushin) is the first step in the Jewish marriage ceremony. Nowadays, the man usually performs אֵירוּסִין by giving the woman a ring in front of two valid witnesses and saying the words: הֲרֵי אַתְּ מְקֻדֶּשֶׁת לִי בְּטַבַּעַת זוֹ כְּדַת מֹשֶׁה וְיִשְׂרָאֵל.

~ see *Sefer HaChinuch, Mitzvah* §552

How do we know that לֹא תִנְאָף refers specifically to a married woman?

A marriage-type relationship between a man and another man's wife is forbidden.

SECTION III

The Laws of the Mitzvah

1. There are two stages to the marriage ceremony, אֵירוּסִין (also known as *kiddushin*) and נִשּׂוּאִין. Once אֵירוּסִין is completed, a woman is considered married, an אֵשֶׁת אִישׁ. A marriage-type relationship between an אֵשֶׁת אִישׁ and a man other than her husband is forbidden.

2. The penalty for violating this prohibition is execution. The violators are put to death by בית דין only if they were warned beforehand that the act was forbidden and that the punishment is death, and only if at least two valid witnesses testified that the man and woman, did indeed, commit the sin. If there were no witnesses, the penalty is כָּרֵת.

3. A woman who commits this *aveirah* is permanently forbidden to both her husband and the man.

4. This prohibition applies to both men and women, in all places and at all times.

5. This act is forbidden to non-Jews as well, as it is included in the prohibition against forbidden relationships, one of the שֶׁבַע מִצְוֹות בְּנֵי נֹחַ.

6. This is one of the three מצוות that a Jew must not violate, even if it means giving up his life (יֵהָרֵג וְאַל יַעֲבוֹר).

7. It is forbidden by Torah law (מִדְּאוֹרַיְתָא) for a man and another man's wife to be alone together in a private place (יִחוּד), as this can lead to adultery. Rabbinically (מִדְּרַבָּנָן), a man may not be alone in a private place even with an unmarried woman, whether she be a Jew or a non-Jew. (This does not apply to some immediate relatives.)

טוב טעם
Appreciating the Mitzvah

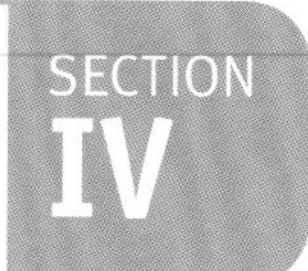

One Who Does This *Aveirah* Denies Hashem

לֹא תִנְאָף, is the second mitzvah on the second לוח of the עשרת הדברות, and it appears directly opposite לֹא יִהְיֶה לְךָ אֱלֹהִים אֲחֵרִים, the second mitzvah on the first לוח. This is to teach us that in Hashem's eyes, one who commits this *aveirah* is like one who recognizes false gods.

~ פסיקתא רבתי §21

A person who commits this *aveirah* thinks that no one knows or sees what he does. He convinces himself that because he performs his evil deeds without anyone's knowledge, Hashem is not aware of him either. He thinks to himself, "No eye will see me." He thinks that no eye below will see him commit his sin, and that the 'Eye' above (Hashem) will not see him either.

~ *Bamidbar Rabbah* 9:1

A person who remembers that Hashem sees and hears everything and that everything we do is recorded in שמים, will not come to do an *aveirah,* as Rabbi Yehudah HaNasi tells us in אבות (2:1): הִסְתַּכֵּל בִּשְׁלֹשָׁה דְבָרִים וְאֵין אַתָּה בָא לִידֵי עֲבֵירָה ... עַיִן רוֹאָה וְאֹזֶן שׁוֹמַעַת וְכָל מַעֲשֶׂיךָ בְּסֵפֶר נִכְתָּבִים, *Keep in mind three things and you will not come to the hands of sin … an Eye that sees, and an Ear that hears, and all your deeds are recorded in a book.*

תשובה Cannot Erase This *Aveirah* Completely

The *aveirah* of לֹא תִנְאָף is truly a terrible one because it produces a result that cannot be undone. As R' Shimon ben Menasyah explains: If a person steals or robs, he can still return the article that he took, and in that way, correct his action. But if one commits adultery with another man's wife, and thereby makes

Did You Know?

In Biblical times, a woman under suspicion of committing this aveirah, would, in certain specific circumstances, be given מֵי הַמָּרִים, the bitter waters, to drink — such a woman is called a סוֹטָה (see במדבר 5:11-31). If she were guilty, she would miraculously die a horrible death; if innocent, she would receive special Divine blessing. There is no other judgment that happens through a miracle except for that of the מֵי הַמָּרִים. Hashem did this to ensure that the kedushah of His nation is never destroyed, or even tainted, by immorality.

~ *Ramban,* במדבר 5:20

A marriage-type relationship between a man and another man's wife is forbidden.

her forbidden to her husband, he can never do complete תְּשׁוּבָה, because he cannot correct the result of his sin. Therefore, his punishment will be especially severe.

~ see *Chagigah* 9b, with *Rashi* and *Maharsha* there; *Tosefta Chagigah* 1:10

שלום בית

When there is *kedushah* in a home, Hashem rests His שכינה in that home. Rashi explains: If a man (איש), and a woman (אשה), are faithful to each other, then Hashem is present, for the י in the word איש and the ה in the word אשה combine to form a Name of Hashem (י–ה). But if they are not, and there is no *kedushah* in their marriage, then the שכינה leaves, and all that is left is אש, *fire,* which consumes them.

~ *Sotah* 17a

The *kedushah* of marriage is enhanced when there is peace and harmony in the house. R' Chelbo taught: A man should be very careful of his wife's honor, for the *berachah* that is found in a man's home is only because of his wife.

~ *Bava Metzia* 59a

When husband and wife live together in harmony and *kedushah,* Hashem blesses the couple with children who are *tzaddikim*, just as Elkanah and Chanah merited having Shmuel HaNavi, who was compared to Moshe Rabbeinu.

~ see *Medrash Tanchuma, Nasso* §7

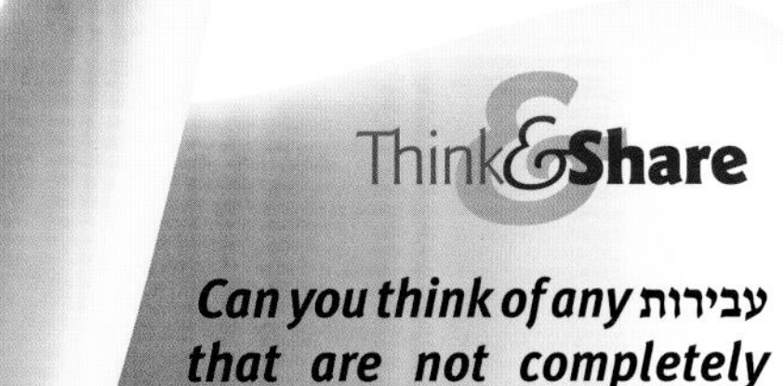

Think&Share

Can you think of any עבירות that are not completely erased by תְּשׁוּבָה alone?

Living the Mitzvah

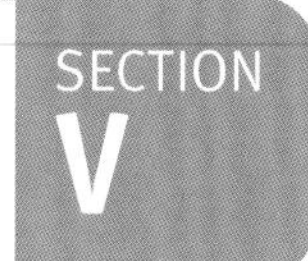

The Missing Fisherman

In this mitzvah we have learned that a married woman cannot have a marriage-type relationship with another man. However, there are two ways in which a marriage can be dissolved, leaving the woman free to marry someone else, as she is no longer an אֵשֶׁת אִישׁ*. If a husband gives his wife a* גֵּט*, a certificate of divorce, the woman is no longer his wife, and she is able to marry another man. Also, if the husband dies and leaves his wife a widow, she is free to marry again.*

A problem arises when a husband disappears and his fate is not known. In such a case, the wife is an agunah (literally: an anchored woman) who is forbidden to remarry until she has clear proof that her husband is dead.

*The Gemara (*יבמות *121a) discusses the law that applies when a husband is lost at sea. The Gemara distinguishes between the case of* מַיִם שֶׁיֵּשׁ לָהֶם סוֹף*, waters that have an end, and* מַיִם שֶׁאֵין לָהֶם סוֹף*, waters that have no end. This means the following: If the husband fell into a body of water small enough that the witness who saw him enter the water could see all of its surrounding shores, and the witness can testify that he saw the man go into the water and that he did not come out, then he is presumed to be dead, and his wife can remarry. But if the body of water "has no end" — that is, it is so large that its shores cannot be seen by the witness, then a witness cannot testify that the husband is definitely dead, for the husband may have come out of the water where the witness could not see him. In such a case, the wife is an agunah and may not remarry.*

The story that follows is based on an incident related in the Gemara, in which a person was lost in "waters that have no end":

Levi and Yissachar set out early on that fateful day. They wanted to claim the best fishing spots before anyone else. They reached the Yarden in good time and picked out what looked like a promising spot. Fishing in the Yarden for these two did not involve poles and

A marriage-type relationship between a man and another man's wife is forbidden.

bait. These men fished with nets. They would wade into the water, then submerge themselves underwater to spread their nets. Once the nets were spread, the fishermen would wait for the fish to enter the nets. They would then pull the nets in, closing them around the fish.

The two men waded into the shallow water and spread their nets. They were having great success, and spent the day busily catching fish. Every so often they moved along the shore to a different spot where there were more fish.

It was late afternoon when they came to a spot where the fish were in great abundance. The sun was starting to set and they would only have enough time for one more catch. Excitedly, they took hold of their nets and waded into the water.

Levi turned to Yissachar and gestured for him to go first. He watched as Yissachar dived into the water to spread his net. Levi stood

and waited to see what his friend would come up with. But Yissachar did not come back up.

It was getting dark and the shadows were lengthening. Levi waited and waited for Yissachar to come up. Nobody could survive that long underwater. Yissachar surely must have drowned! With a heavy heart, Levi started for home. He would have to break the terrible news to Yissachar's wife and children.

Yissachar, however, was alive and well. Unbeknownst to Levi, there was an underground cave that the fish had burrowed into, creating an entrance into it. Yissachar swam into the hole to see if he could spread his net there. Once inside, he discovered that the top of the tunnel was not underwater, and he was able to stand up and breathe. He was having great success with his fishing, and lost track of time. However, the tunnel became darker and darker, and as the sun set, it became pitch black. Yissachar could not see his way out of the tunnel in the dark, so he was forced to spend a dark, cold, wet night alone in the cave, waiting for morning to arrive.

Levi broke the tragic news to Yissachar's wife. Her husband would not be coming home tonight, or any other night. Shocked

A marriage-type relationship between a man and another man's wife is forbidden.

and grief-stricken, she burst into sobs. With a broken heart, she told her family and friends of her husband's death, and prepared to hold a *hesped* (eulogy) the next day.

After a long, tear-filled night, Yissachar's family gathered together to memorialize their dear relative. Eulogies were delivered and anecdotes and stories were told. All of Yissachar's friends and family had gathered to say goodbye.

Yissachar, meanwhile, had never been so thankful for the sun. As it rose in the sky, enough light came into the tunnel that Yissachar was able to make his way out. He started on his way home.

As Yissachar neared his house, he saw that his yard was filled with people. As he drew closer, he heard the sounds of crying. As he entered his yard and started to make his way to his front door, the people just turned and stared at him. They made way for him and a path opened up for him. He walked in through the front door and stopped. There sat his dear wife and children, sobbing, while one of his relatives was delivering a speech about him.

"Oh my!" thought Yissachar, "they thought I was dead! This is my *hesped*. They have pronounced me dead, and my dear wife a widow!"

Just then Yissachar's wife looked up and saw who was standing in the doorway. To her utter amazement, it was her husband!

When this story reached the ears of Rebbi, Rabbi Yehudah HaNasi, he exclaimed, "How great are the words of the Sages, who said that if one is lost in waters that have an end, his wife is allowed to remarry, but if he is lost in waters that have *no* end, his wife is forbidden to remarry."

This story serves as a perfect example of the above. Levi assumed that Yissachar was dead because he did not know about the tunnel. Since the Yarden is a body of water that has no end, meaning that it is so large that a person cannot see all the surrounding shores, Levi should never have assumed that Yissachar had perished. He made a mistake by presuming Yissachar to be dead, and if Yissachar's wife had remarried, she would have violated the prohibition of לֹא תִנְאָף.

FOCUS

Why can't a witness who saw a man go into "waters that have no end" testify that he is dead?

Expand Your Knowledge

SECTION VI

Yosef HaTzaddik and Potifar's Wife:

In פרשת פנחס (במדבר ch. 26), when the Jewish people are counted, the Torah adds the Name of Hashem, י–ה, to each family's name (for example, the family of חֲנוֹךְ is called **הַחֲנֹכִי**). Rashi explains that this is Hashem's testimony that Bnei Yisrael did not get caught in the net of immorality that was Mitzrayim. They remained pure and holy, keeping the *kedushah* of the Jewish marriage alive. In all the time Bnei Yisrael were in Mitzrayim, surrounded by the Egyptians' sinful behavior, Bnei Yisrael kept themselves separate and did not fall into the depraved ways of Egyptian society.

Where did Bnei Yisrael find the strength to remain unaffected by Egyptian culture?

Chazal tell us that it is because of Yosef HaTzaddik. Yosef refused to sin with Potifar's wife, who set her sights upon him. Every day, she would come to Yosef and try to get him to sin with her. Yosef always refused her. Even when he was tempted, he withstood the test. He saw the image of his father Yaakov in front of him, and strengthened himself against sinning. Potifar's wife finally had enough. She accused Yosef of sinning, and Yosef, though innocent, was thrown into jail.

Because Yosef withstood this test, he instilled within Bnei Yisrael the strength to withstand tests of immorality. In this merit alone, Bnei Yisrael deserved to be redeemed from Mitzrayim.

~ *Vayikra Rabbah* 32:5

Determine Mastery

REVIEWING KEY INFORMATION

1. What are the three מצוות for which a person must sacrifice his life rather than violate (יהרג ואל יעבור)?
2. Why is it impossible to do complete תְּשׁוּבָה for this עבירה?
3. How does a person who commits this aveirah deny Hashem's existence?
4. What two occurrences can halachically end a marriage?

CRITICAL THINKING

1. Why is שְׁלוֹם בַּיִת such an essential part of the Jewish home?

In loving memory of

Nathan Rothner ע"ה

Chicago / Jerusalem

מצוה

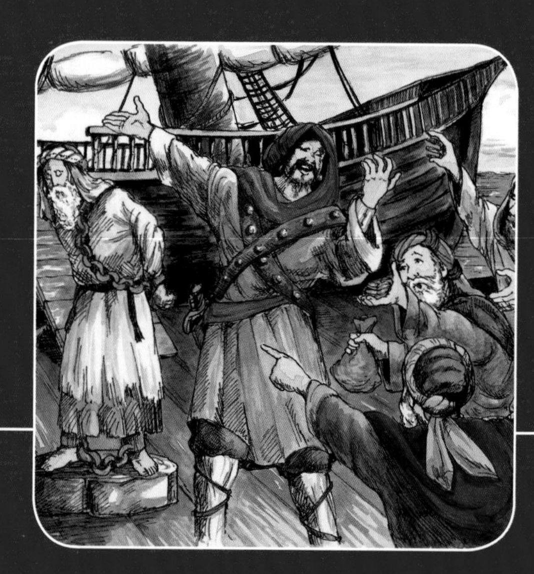

MITZVAH 36

Do Not Kidnap

איסור גניבת נפש

MITZVAH **36**

איסור גניבת נפש

Do Not Kidnap

THE MITZVAH

It is forbidden to seize a person and take possession of him against his will.

- בְּחִירָה
- לְשֵׁם שָׁמַיִם
- עֶבֶד כְּנַעֲנִי
- וּבֹזִי
- יֵקָלוּ
- אֵבֶר מִן הַחַי

SECTION I Introduction to the Mitzvah

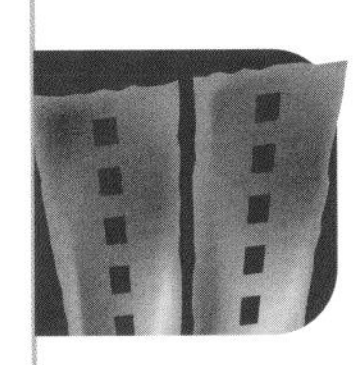

Once there was a mighty king who ruled over a vast empire. One day, the king selected one family from among his subjects and gave them a special job. The members of this family were to devote their lives to a single purpose — serving the king and fulfilling his every wish.

Would anyone dare to kidnap a member of this family and make him his personal slave? Is there any doubt that if he did, the king would punish him severely?

One who kidnaps another Jew is seizing a special servant of the King of the universe. Every Jew is a servant devoted to the royal service of Hashem, as the Torah states (ויקרא 25:42): עֲבָדַי הֵם אֲשֶׁר הוֹצֵאתִי אֹתָם מֵאֶרֶץ מִצְרָיִם, *They are My servants, whom I have taken out of the land of Egypt.* "They are My servants," says Hashem, "and are not to be servants to other servants."

~ *Derech Pikudecha,* לא תעשה §36

A Jew is created בְּצֶלֶם אֱלֹקִים (*in the Divine Image*), and must guide his own life by using בְּחִירָה (*free will*). When he is kidnapped, he loses the ability to do this. By denying his victim this right, the kidnapper ignores the existence of his victim's צֶלֶם אֱלֹקִים.

~ *Recanti* in טעמי המצוות, לא תעשה §21

Think & Share

The Torah prohibits kidnapping using the verb תִּגְנֹב, a verb which usually refers to theft done secretly. Why would the Torah choose to use this verb here?

The Source of the Mitzvah

SECTION II

לֹא תִגְנֹב

שמות כ:יג פרשת יתרו

Do not steal

In the עשרת הדברות, לֹא תִגְנֹב comes immediately after לֹא תִרְצָח (*Do not murder*) and לֹא תִנְאָף (*Do not commit adultery*). This teaches us that just as לֹא תִרְצָח and לֹא תִנְאָף are sins for which the sinner is sentenced to death, so, too, לֹא תִגְנֹב is a sin punishable by death. Now, a person who steals another person's possessions does not receive the death penalty. Therefore, the פסוק of לֹא תִגְנֹב cannot be referring to the stealing of possessions. However, elsewhere in the Torah (שמות 21:16) we learn that a kidnapper does receive the death penalty. Therefore, we see that לֹא תִגְנֹב in the עשרת הדברות must be forbidding the kidnapping of another human being, rather than the stealing of possessions. Theft of property is prohibited by another פסוק, לֹא תִגְנֹבוּ, which appears in פרשת קדושים (ויקרא 19:11).

~ *Mechilta*, שמות 20:14

Did You Know?

A person can be guilty of "enslaving" another's soul even without actually kidnapping him or making him into a servant. A person should never act in a way that will cause others to fear him (unless he is doing so לְשֵׁם שָׁמַיִם, for the sake of Heaven). A servant of Hashem should have no cause to fear anyone but Hashem. Each person must always be treated with dignity, in a way that enhances his self-respect, and not in a way that will cause him to fear others.

~ *Shaarei Teshuvah* 3:167

How do we know that לא תגנב in the עשרת הדברות refers to kidnapping and not to stealing another person's property?

It is forbidden to seize a person and take possession of him against his will.

SECTION III

The Laws of the Mitzvah

1. A person is guilty of kidnapping only when he takes the victim into his own domain, such as his house, his land, his boat, etc. As soon as he does this, he has violated the prohibition of לֹא תִּגְנֹב and is liable to punishment.

2. A person is not allowed to kidnap anyone: man, woman, or child.

3. A kidnapper is liable to the death penalty only if a) he took his victim into his own domain, *and* b) he physically used his victim (even for a relatively minor use, such as leaning on him), *and* c) in the end, he sold his victim in the manner that one sells an עֶבֶד כְּנַעֲנִי. Such a kidnapper will receive the death penalty of strangulation (חֶנֶק) if convicted by בית דין, as long as he was warned beforehand (הַתְרָאָה) that he would be killed for committing this crime and two valid witnesses testified that he did, in fact, do so.

4. This prohibition applies to both men and women, in all places and at all times. As a general rule, all of the Torah's prohibitions (מצוות לא תעשה) apply equally to men and women.

5. Non-Jews are forbidden to kidnap as well. This is because kidnapping is included in the prohibition against theft, which is one of the שֶׁבַע מִצְוֹות בְּנֵי נֹחַ.

6. A person who kidnaps another person who is easily accessible to him, such as his son or his student, has violated this prohibition, but does not receive the death penalty. This is true even if the kidnapper has fulfilled all three of the conditions (see Law 3) needed for בית דין to sentence him to death.

MITZVAH 25
MITZVAH 26
MITZVAH 27
MITZVAH 28
MITZVAH 29
MITZVAH 30
MITZVAH 31
MITZVAH 32
MITZVAH 33
MITZVAH 34
MITZVAH 35
MITZVAH 36
MITZVAH 37
MITZVAH 38

טוב טעם
Appreciating the Mitzvah

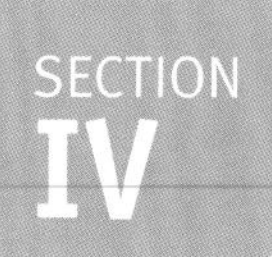
SECTION IV

Harm to the Victim's גוף and נשמה

To kidnap a person is to strip him of a most basic right — the right to be free.

~ see *R' Samson Raphael Hirsch* to שמות 20:13 and 21:16

Kidnapping tears the victim away from his home and everything that is familiar to him. If he is sold as a slave to a severe taskmaster, he is liable to be beaten, perhaps even to death, when he fails to perform as expected.

~ see בבא בתרא 8b

Perhaps even greater than the damage done to the victim's body is the damage done to his נשמה. The transformation of a proud, free man into a captive slave harms the victim spiritually as well. The task of a free man is to serve Hashem. If a person is kidnapped and sold to someone who will have little sympathy for his religious observance, the spiritual danger is obvious. In such cases, the kidnapper has caused his victim more harm than he would have by killing him — for he has deprived him not only of his quality of life in this world, but also eternal life in the next.

~ see *Meshech Chochmah,* דברים 24:7

Harm to Society

The act of kidnapping is more than just an offense against one individual. It attacks the very foundation of our civilization that allows people to live peacefully with one another. Therefore, the Torah considers kidnapping a capital crime, punishable by death. In an environment where basic human rights are ignored, no individual is safe.

~ ספר הברית II 13:13

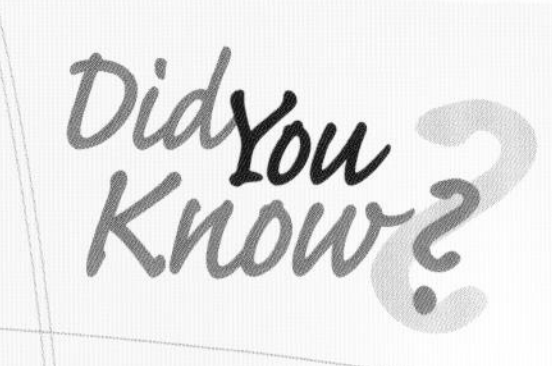

In the end, if the kidnapper does sell his victim as if he was an עֶבֶד כְּנַעֲנִי, the sale is not valid, for the kidnapper has no right to sell him! Nevertheless, the kidnapper has also violated Mitzvah 345, לֹא יִמָּכְרוּ מִמְכֶּרֶת עָבֶד, for even attempting to sell him in such a manner.

~ מנחת חינוך 36:6

It is forbidden to seize a person and take possession of him against his will.

Harm to the Victim's *Mesorah*

The parent-child relationship is basic to human society, and especially to the Jewish people. Our Torah, along with its rich traditions and customs, is handed down lovingly and faithfully from generation to generation, from parent to child. A kidnapper breaks the chain of transmission, the *mesorah,* by stealing the victim away from his family, and this alone is a most serious crime.

"Those Who Honor Me..."

When a kidnapper robs others of their freedom and treats them shamefully, he is harming himself as well.

The Mishnah (אבות 4:1) teaches: אֵיזֶהוּ מְכֻבָּד הַמְכַבֵּד אֶת הַבְּרִיּוֹת, *Who deserves honor? A person who honors others.* It is written (*Shmuel* I 2:30): כִּי מְכַבְּדַי אֲכַבֵּד וּבֹזַי יֵקָלּוּ, *Those who honor Me, I will honor; but those who disgrace Me, will be shamed.*

When we honor others, we are showing that we recognize the צלם אלקים within them. By honoring them, we are actually honoring Hashem, Who placed within each one of us a holy נשמה. By honoring others, we are accomplishing the opposite of what a kidnapper does. Instead of degrading souls, we uplift them and build self-esteem. A person who honors others truly deserves honor.

FOCUS

In what ways does a kidnapper harm himself?

Living the Mitzvah

The Four Captives

The following story is based on a famous episode in Jewish history.

Kidnapping is a most serious crime. Stealing a possession may cause the victim great loss, and the robber must repay double what he stole. How much greater is the loss and the suffering caused by kidnapping a person! When a kidnapper commits this terrible act, his motive may be that he wants to destroy his victim's life without murdering him; he may want to degrade him and cause him great suffering. Another common motive for kidnapping is to make money; the kidnapper sells his victims to the highest bidder. The following story illustrates this:

The pirate, Ibn Rumahis, laughed as he refilled his mug. It had been a very profitable day and his crew deserved a reward. They had just sold the last of their slaves for a very good price. It was extremely rewarding, monetarily that is, to be captain of your very own pirate vessel. Their latest venture was attacking other ships, but not only for the gold and silver. Now they were kidnapping every last passenger and crew member and selling them as slaves. Of course, it was tricky. You didn't want to get caught. The price for kidnapping and dealing in the slave trade was your head. But it was too profitable to give up. The Jews were worth the most, of course. Their brethren would always buy any Jewish captives from him, even at great cost.

"Those Jews are good for something," thought Ibn Rumahis — "filling my pockets with gold!"

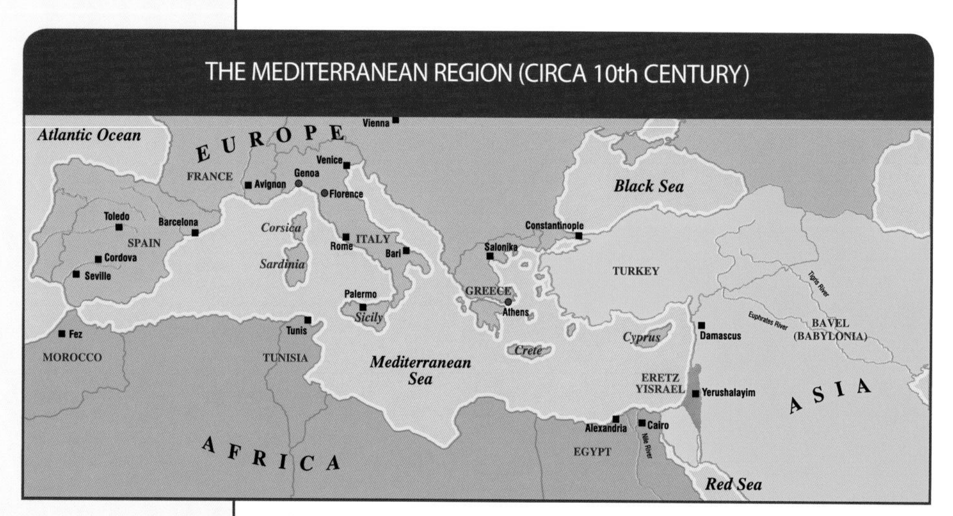

■ Cities and Towns with Large Jewish Communities ● Other Major Cities

The captain was enjoying his drink, the wind blowing the salty air in his face. He was just about to retire for the night when his lookout cried out. "A ship! Captain, there is a ship on the horizon, dead ahead. She looks to be a passenger ship."

It is forbidden to seize a person and take possession of him against his will.

"How lucky," thought the captain. "Fortune has smiled on us again." Quickly, he shouted to the helmsman, "Hold your course steady, Daoud. Let's pay that ship a visit, shall we?"

"Aye, Captain," replied the helmsman. "We should reach the other ship in a few hours."

"Wonderful," said the captain. "I'll be in my quarters."

On the other ship, the passengers were enjoying the calm seas.

"How many days until we reach home, Father?" asked Chanoch, the son of R' Moshe.

"I do not know," replied his father. "Hashem will guide us."

Four outstanding תלמידי חכמים and their families had been sent from Bavel (Babylon) on a fund-raising expedition. The Torah centers in Bavel were a long way from most of the Jewish areas of settlement. The Jews were spreading out all over Europe and Africa, anywhere where they could find peace for a little while. These scholars, R' Moshe ben Chanoch, R' Chushiel, R' Shemaryah ben Elchanan, and a fourth whose name has been lost from the pages of history, were sent to raise money for *tzedakah*. They had completed their task successfully and were now sailing home from Bari, Italy.

"Look, Father, there is another ship heading our way! It's coming right at us!" cried Chanoch.

It was the pirate ship, heading straight for them. Suddenly, panicked cries arose from the crew. "It's the ship of Ibn Rumahis! Help us! We are all doomed!"

Indeed, there was nowhere to go on the open seas. They could not outrun the pirate ship.

The pirate ship drew up alongside the other vessel. The pirates boarded the passenger ship, swords drawn. The crew defended the ship and her passengers valiantly, but they were no match for the ruthless pirates, who did not hesitate to cut down anyone who stood in their way.

The rest of the crew and the passengers were rounded up, while other pirates went searching for gold, silver, jewels, and whatever merchandise the ship was carrying. Quickly, the pirates gathered everything together.

The pirate captain looked over all the jewels and finery his crew had found. "Well done, men. We are now richer than ten sheiks." Then he

surveyed the prisoners. When he spotted the Jews, his eyes lit up with a greedy gleam. Before him was a fortune! The Jewish communities would pay dearly for these men and their families. If this wasn't so much fun, he could even retire!

He ordered all the loot and the captives to be transferred to his ship, with special orders to put the Jews in a separate cell. These commands were quickly carried out. The first ship lay in the middle of the ocean, abandoned. Eventually, some other ship would come across her and know her sad fate.

The prisoners, locked up in their dank and dirty cells, knew that a terrible fate awaited them. They were now in the clutches of murderous thieves who would think nothing of killing them all if they could not get a good price for them on the auction block. Their lives were now worth only what the pirates could get for them. Not only had they been stripped of all their possessions, they had lost their freedom as well. The Jewish prisoners sat together in their cell and prayed to their true Master to free them from their dire situation.

It is forbidden to seize a person and take possession of him against his will.

Meanwhile, the captain and the crew were again celebrating their good fortune. However, the captain was not drinking this time. He needed a clear head. He wanted to figure out which communities would pay the most for his Jewish captives. Of course, he would not sell them all to one community. He could get more for each of them individually. Cunningly he made his plan, and immediately gave the order to set sail for Alexandria, Egypt.

When the ship reached port, the captain immediately sent a message to the delegates of the Jewish community. He told the delegates that he had a prisoner they might be interested in buying, and he demanded an exorbitant sum. The delegates told the captain that they must first see the captive before they entered into any negotiations. The captain laughed and allowed them to meet R' Shemaryah ben Elchanan. After all, he knew that the Jews would not leave any of their kind behind. When the delegates met R' Shemaryah, they realized just what kind of Torah scholar stood before them. They told R' Shemaryah that they would pay any price for him, and asked him to be their leader. Scholars of his caliber did not come their way every day. R' Shemaryah agreed and the deal was struck.

The same scene played out in Tunis, Tunisia where R' Chushiel was redeemed; in Cordova, Spain, where R' Moshe ben Chanoch and his son, Chanoch, were redeemed; and again in another port, where the fourth captive was redeemed.

These scholars became leaders of Sephardic Jewry. As the settlements of the Jews shifted, the locations of יְשִׁיבוֹת and the scholars they produced shifted as well. With the freeing of these four scholars and their redemption by the various settlements outside of Bavel, the flame of Torah never wavered, and the survival of Torah was ensured. Through Hashem's Providence, the era of the Rishonim had begun.

Even though the Jewish captives were redeemed, and they each became leaders of their new communities, this did not absolve Ibn Rumahis and his cohorts from the terrible sin of kidnapping. They had caused much pain and suffering to the four scholars and to all those who were prisoners aboard their ship.

Think & **Share**

Why should the pirates be held accountable for something which actually ensured the survival of Torah?

Expand Your Knowledge

SECTION VI

The שֶׁבַע מִצְוֹות בְּנֵי נֹחַ

Non-Jews are required to keep seven מצוות. These מצוות are called the שבע מצוות בני נח because they apply to the descendants of Noach and his family, who were the sole survivors of the מבול.

The seven מצוות are:

1. Non-Jews are required to establish a system of courts and civil law.
2. They are forbidden to "bless" (this actually refers to the opposite of blessing) the Name of Hashem. [This sin is so terrible that Chazal never state it openly.]
3. They may not worship idols.
4. They may not have forbidden relationships (such as adultery).
5. They may not murder.
6. They may not steal (kidnapping is included in this prohibition).
7. They may not eat a limb torn from a live animal (אֵבֶר מִן הַחַי).

Applying Your Knowledge:

One of the most tragic episodes in the Torah was the kidnapping of Dinah, the daughter of Yaakov, by Shechem, the son of Chamor, a non-Jew. According to one opinion, Shechem was deserving of death for kidnapping Dinah (see 6 above), and his fellow citizens were deserving of death for not trying him in court and giving him his just punishment (see 1 above). This is why Shimon and Levi attacked and killed the people of that city.

~ *Rambam*, הלכות מלכים 9:14

Determine Mastery

REVIEWING KEY INFORMATION

1. How does a kidnapper ignore the צלם אלקים of his victim?
2. What must the kidnapper do in order for בית דין to sentence him to death?
3. How is a kidnapper executed by בית דין?
4. How does a kidnapper bring harm to both the victim's גוף and נשמה?
5. How is society affected by the actions of a kidnapper?

CRITICAL THINKING

1. What does the verse עֲבָדַי הֵם אֲשֶׁר הוֹצֵאתִי אֹתָם מֵאֶרֶץ מִצְרָיִם have to do with לֹא תִגְנֹב?

לע"נ
נסים רחמים בן סמבול ע"ה

The Rudy Family

מצוה

37

MITZVAH

Do Not Testify Falsely

איסור עדות שקר

MITZVAH 37

איסור עדות שקר

Do Not Testify Falsely

THE MITZVAH

It is forbidden to give false testimony, or to testify that one saw an incident happen if he did not personally witness it, even if he heard about the incident from reliable sources.

- אֱמֶת
- קַיָּם
- שֶׁקֶר
- לֹא תַעֲנֶה
- זוֹמְמִים
- נִצָּב
- עֲדַת
- בְּקֶרֶב
- נֶאֱמָן

SECTION I — Introduction to the Mitzvah

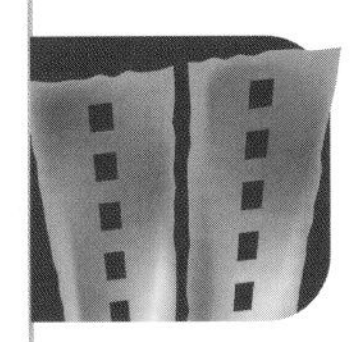

Did you know that each king has a unique seal? Over the centuries, the kings and queens of England, France, and other countries have had their own seals. Even the president of the United States has his own seal. The seal of a world leader is very symbolic.

A king's seal is the stamp that represents him and his kingdom. The Gemara (שבת 55a) tells us that the seal of Hashem is אֱמֶת. A person who truly desires to follow in Hashem's ways must always speak the truth and act truthfully in all situations.

To lie in court is an especially evil form of שקר, *falsehood*. The Mishnah (אבות 1:18) teaches, עַל שְׁלֹשָׁה דְּבָרִים הָעוֹלָם קַיָּם עַל הַדִּין וְעַל הָאֱמֶת וְעַל הַשָּׁלוֹם, *The world endures on three things: justice, truth, and peace.* In order for society to survive, there must be a judicial system with laws and courts. This system of justice depends upon the accurate testimony of witnesses to help the judges determine the truth about disputed events. This helps them arrive at decisions that are just and fair. A false witness corrupts the legal process, and makes it impossible for the court to issue correct judgments. False witnesses undermine the very foundations of society.

On the other hand, witnesses who are faithful to the truth and come forward to provide בית דין with the information it needs, are performing a mitzvah and upholding the world.

~ *Chinuch* §37

Why is אמת an appropriate seal for Hashem, the King of kings?

The Source of the Mitzvah

SECTION II

לֹא תַעֲנֶה בְרֵעֲךָ עֵד שָׁקֶר

שמות כ:יג פרשת יתרו

Do not bear false witness against your fellow

The פסוק states: לֹא תַעֲנֶה בְרֵעֲךָ עֵד שָׁקֶר, *You shall not bear false witness against your fellow.* Based on the wording of the פסוק, some authorities maintain that only false testimony *against* another person is included in this prohibition. For example, if Reuven testified that Shimon committed an act that בית דין will have to punish him for having done, or that Shimon borrowed money from Levi and must repay it, then Reuven has violated the prohibition of לֹא תַעֲנֶה. However, if Reuven testified that Shimon did *not* commit a crime, or if he offered testimony that does not cause harm to another person (such as testifying that he saw the new moon on the thirtieth day of the month), Reuven would not violate this prohibition.

~ תשובות R' Akiva Eiger, מהדורא קמא §176 ד"ה הדברים רחוקים, מהדורא בתרא §47

Other authorities disagree, and say that the prohibition applies to testimony that *affects* another person, even if the testimony is not directed *against* a person. According to these authorities, this prohibition does include testimony regarding the proper day to establish Rosh Chodesh, since this affects all Jews.

~ *Kovetz Shiurim,* בבא בתרא §328, מנחת חינוך 4:13

Did You Know?

Even if it is clear that a witness is telling the truth, his testimony is not always accepted. Any relative who is closely related to either of the parties involved in a court case, even if he is a tzaddik who would never lie, is not a valid witness and is not qualified to testify.

~ see בבא בתרא 159a

There is, in fact, a separate mitzvah, Mitzvah 589, that prohibits בית דין to accept testimony from this person.

Reading Check

Does a witness who testifies falsely that he saw the new moon violate לֹא תַעֲנֶה?

It is forbidden to give false testimony, or to testify that one saw an incident happen if he did not personally witness it, even if he heard about the incident from reliable sources.

SECTION III The Laws of the Mitzvah

1. A person is not allowed to give false testimony against his fellow Jew, whether that testimony is given orally in בית דין or by signing as a [false] witness on a document.

2. A person is forbidden to make up false testimony even to prove a claim that he knows is true.

3. A person violates this prohibition only if בית דין would act upon his testimony. Therefore, if a single witness testifies falsely by himself where two witnesses are needed, he does not violate this prohibition. But if he testifies together with a valid witness, he does violate this prohibition, because בית דין would act upon his testimony.

4. This prohibition applies only to testimony given in בית דין.

5. This prohibition applies at all times to men but not to women, as women generally do not testify in בית דין.

6. The punishment for transgressing this prohibition is מַלְקוּת, *lashes*. Unlike most cases, violators of this לא תעשה receive מַלְקוּת even though they were not warned and committed no physical action.

7. There is a special category of false witnesses known as עֵדִים זוֹמְמִים. Witnesses become עֵדִים זוֹמְמִים only if the following occurs: Two witnesses give false testimony in בית דין that they saw a certain incident happen; then a second set of witnesses testifies that the first witnesses could not have seen the incident happen, because the first witnesses were with them in a different place at the time the incident supposedly occurred. The first witnesses are called עֵדִים זוֹמְמִים, and are subject to special punishment (see Mitzvah 524).

Note: When witnesses offer true testimony in בית דין, they fulfill a mitzvah (see Mitzvah 122).

טוב טעם
Appreciating the Mitzvah

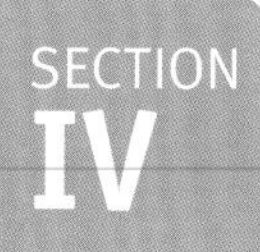

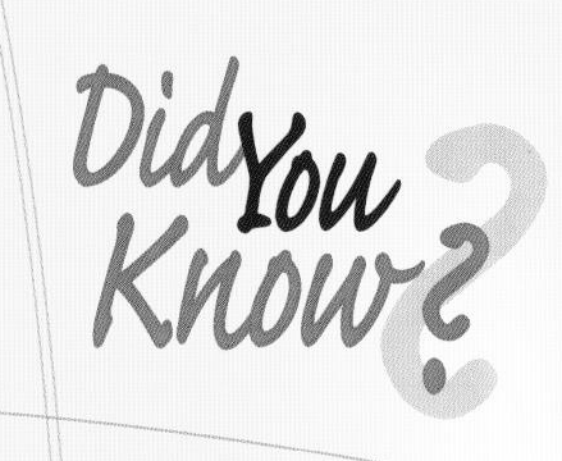

Shlomo HaMelech had a very special throne. Different animals lined each side of the steps leading up to the king's seat. When false witnesses appeared before the king, the gears of the throne, which were created with wisdom, would start spinning and the golden animals would start to roar and shriek. All this was to strike fear in the hearts of the witnesses and to stop them from lying.

~ *Targum Sheni* to מגילת אסתר 1:2

☙ The False Witness Disregards Hashem's Presence

Hashem rests His Presence, His שכינה, upon a Torah court of law (בית דין), and involves Himself in the legal process, as it says (*Tehillim* 82:1): אֱלֹקִים נִצָּב בַּעֲדַת קֵל בְּקֶרֶב אֱלֹהִים יִשְׁפֹּט, *Hashem stands in the Divine assembly; in the midst of judges shall He judge.*

A person who presents himself before a בית דין and testifies falsely shows that not only does he not care about truth and justice, but he does not care (or does not believe) that Hashem's שכינה is present.

~ *R' Menachem HaBavli*

In fact, this wording of the prohibition reflects this part of the liar's crime. The Torah states, לֹא תַעֲנֶה בְרֵעֲךָ עֵד שָׁקֶר, *Do not bear false witness against your fellow.* Hashem can also be referred to as man's fellow, as it is written (*Mishlei* 27:10), רֵעֲךָ וְרֵעַ אָבִיךָ אַל תַּעֲזֹב, *Your Fellow (Hashem) and the Fellow of your father you shall not abandon.* Therefore, the פסוק can be understood as stating: One who testifies falsely does so not only against his fellow man, but also against his Fellow in Heaven, Hashem.

~ *Recanti* in טעמי המצוות, לא תעשה §23

☙ The False Witness Denies Hashem's Power

Hashem is אמת, and His seal is אמת. Therefore, any falsehood in the world contradicts the belief that Hashem created it.

The Talmud Yerushalmi (ברכות 1:5) says in the name of Rabbi Levi: Hashem declares, "If you dare to testify falsely against your friend, I will consider it as if you testified that I did not create the world."

Additionally, a faithful Jew knows that whatever happens in this world is decreed by Hashem, including exactly how much a

It is forbidden to give false testimony, or to testify that one saw an incident happen if he did not personally witness it, even if he heard about the incident from reliable sources.

person will earn each year. Hashem decrees every Rosh Hashanah how much money a person will receive in the coming year, and no one can change this.

~ see *Beitzah* 17a

A false witness shows that he does not believe this. As an example, let us examine a case where a false witness testifies to force someone to pay money that he does not really owe. The witness believes that it is in his power to take money away from its rightful owner and give it to the person who hired him to lie. Of course, this is not so. Only Hashem decides how much money each person is supposed to have.

מדבר שקר תרחק

The word אמת is made up of the first, middle, and last letters of the אלף-בית. It is also made up of the first letter in the עשרת הדברות (א, from אנכי), the first letter in the Mishnah (מ, from מֵאֵימָתַי), and the first letter in the Gemara (ת, from תַּנָּא). This teaches us that the Torah is אמת, and in order to live a life of Torah, we must also live a life of truth. Hashem is אמת, and we must always strive to be like Hashem in every way. אמת should always be on our lips.

In fact, because it is so easy for a person to alter the truth if he is not careful, the Torah warns us (שמות 23:7) מִדְּבַר שֶׁקֶר תִּרְחָק, *Keep far away from a false word*. We must not stray from the truth even a little bit.

If we always strive to stay on the path of אמת, we will be sure to always avoid saying a false word, and certainly we will never come to testify falsely.

FOCUS

What is a false witness showing that he does not believe in when he lies in court?

Living the Mitzvah

SECTION V

Saved by the Vilna Gaon

As we have learned, שקר is a terrible thing. When false witnesses come forward to testify in בית דין, not only are they committing the terrible act of lying, but they can cause an innocent person unjust harm, as almost happened in the story below.

The city of Vilna was in an uproar. The news was on everyone's lips. The child of one of the most prominent men of the city had been accused of committing a terrible crime! The residents of the city could not believe what they were hearing. How could such a thing be true?

Two witnesses had come forward and had appeared before the city's בית דין. They had presented their testimony in full detail. The judges had examined and cross-examined the witnesses thoroughly, and they could find no weakness in their testimonies. It seemed quite clear that the witnesses were telling the truth, and that the young woman was guilty and would have to face the consequences of her crime.

R' Eliyahu of Vilna, better known as the Vilna Gaon, rarely left his study. There, day and night, he immersed himself in the study of

It is forbidden to give false testimony, or to testify that one saw an incident happen if he did not personally witness it, even if he heard about the incident from reliable sources.

Torah. But when an urgent matter needed his attention, the Gaon's talmidim made sure that he was kept well-informed. Now, as this fine Jewish daughter stood accused of a terrible crime and was facing dire punishment, the בית דין consulted with the Gaon, and told him all the details of the case.

When the בית דין finished relating all the details, R' Eliyahu reflected on all the information. With his keen insight and greatness of spirit, the Gaon suspected that the young woman was being falsely accused. He would go to court in person.

R' Eliyahu made his way to the בית דין and requested that the judges question the witnesses again, this time in his presence. The witnesses were called in, one at a time, and repeated what they had said earlier.

Again and again, R' Eliyahu asked the judges to question the witnesses. And each time, each witness' testimony was exactly the same. Not only that, but both witnesses told the exact same story. Every detail was identical. There was not the slightest discrepancy between the two testimonies, no matter how many times they had to repeat it.

The Vilna Gaon listened intently to every word. After yet another cross-examination was completed, he suddenly pointed to the witnesses and thundered, "They are false witnesses!"

The witnesses turned pale. The judges and everyone present were stunned. The witnesses were very frightened, and suddenly broke down and confessed that they had made up the whole story. In the face of the great *tzaddik* calling them liars, they were not able to stick to their lies.

The Vilna Gaon, satisfied that true justice would be done, left the courtroom to return to his study.

Outside the courtroom, however, he was besieged by his students, who all asked him to explain how he had known that the witnesses were lying. The Vilna Gaon explained how he had known that they were, indeed, false witnesses:

"The Mishnah (*Sanhedrin* 5:4) states that the judges in a case should hear the testimony of each witness separately. First, they call in one witness without the other present and question him. Then they do the same to the second witness. In this way they can determine אִם נִמְצְאוּ דִבְרֵיהֶם מְכֻוָּנִין, *if their words were found to be in agreement.*

The Mishnah uses the word נמצאו, ***found to be*** in agreement. We can ask: Why didn't the Mishnah just say, אִם הָיוּ דִבְרֵיהֶם מְכֻוָּנִין, *if their words **were** in agreement?*"

It is forbidden to give false testimony, or to testify that one saw an incident happen if he did not personally witness it, even if he heard about the incident from reliable sources.

The Vilna Gaon went on to explain: "The testimony of two witnesses should not be absolutely identical. Two people who witness the same scene always describe it somewhat differently. No two people view something in exactly the same way.

In fact, if the two accounts are *exactly* identical, then there is cause for concern. This should raise our suspicions that the two witnesses plotted together, prepared a fabricated story, rehearsed it over and over until they got it just right, and then presented it from memory in the courtroom.

This is why the Mishnah states: *If their words are found to be in agreement.* The witnesses' testimony should not match perfectly. Rather, it is up to the judges to compare the two testimonies and decide if they are similar enough to be "found" in agreement.

When I heard the two witnesses in the courtroom repeat their testimonies," the Gaon concluded, "I realized that their accounts did not differ by even a single word. Each time they repeated the story, the accounts remained exactly the same. That is how I knew they were false witnesses."

Because of the Vilna Gaon's great insight and wisdom, the plot of the two false witnesses was uncovered, and an innocent בת ישראל was saved from a terrible punishment.

What does this story teach us about how precisely all of the Torah, including תורה שבעל פה, is worded?

Expand Your Knowledge

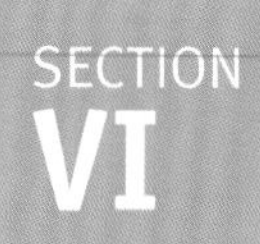

When the Testimony of Only One Witness Is Acceptable

In capital or monetary cases, the Torah requires a minimum of two valid witnesses (see Mitzvah 523 — לֹא יָקוּם עֵד אֶחָד בְּאִישׁ). However, there are other cases where the testimony of even a single witness is sufficient. In these cases, if a single witness testifies falsely, he violates the prohibition of לא תענה, as his testimony would be accepted by בית דין.

Some instances where the testimony of a single witness is accepted are:

1 A single witness can testify that a husband has died, thereby allowing his widow to remarry.

~ *Mishnah,* **יבמות** 117b

2 If a Jew is found murdered in Eretz Yisrael and the identity of the murderer is unknown, the Torah requires that the בית דין of the city closest to the place where the body was found perform the עֶגְלָה עֲרוּפָה ritual (see Mitzvah 530 and Mitzvah 531). If even a single witness testifies to the identity of the murderer, then the בית דין does not perform the ritual (even though the murderer cannot be convicted, since there is only one witness).

~ *Sotah* 47b; *Rambam,* **הלכות עדות** 5:2

3 If a single witness testifies that Reuven owes Shimon money, Reuven is not obligated to pay. However, based on the single witness' testimony, Reuven does have to swear in בית דין that he does not owe Shimon the money.

~ *Rambam,* **הלכות טוען ונטען** 3:6

There is a rule that עֵד אֶחָד נֶאֱמָן בְּאִסוּרִין, *a single witness is believed with respect to whether an item is forbidden or permitted.* For example, a single witness is believed to testify that a particular food is kosher. The authorities disagree as to whether a person who testifies falsely about such matters violates לא תענה.

~ see *Gittin* 2b

Determine Mastery

REVIEWING KEY INFORMATION

1. How do false witnesses endanger the continued existence of the world?
2. When does a witness who testifies falsely not violate לֹא תַעֲנֶה?
3. What is the punishment for violating לֹא תַעֲנֶה?
4. How does a false witness show that he has no regard for Hashem's honor?
5. How did the Vilna Gaon deduce from a Mishnah that the witnesses must be lying?
6. In what instances will the testimony of a single witness be accepted?

CRITICAL THINKING

1. How can a witness ever be proven false, if בית דין always accepts the testimony of two witnesses to be absolutely true?
2. Explain: מִדְּבַר שֶׁקֶר תִּרְחָק.

לע"נ ר' אריה לייב בן ר' יוסף ז"ל
לע"נ חיה לאה בת ר' חיים יעקב ז"ל
למשפחת לנסברג

Dave and Judy Landsberg
Effy and Tzivie Landsberg

מצוה

לח

MITZVAH

38

Do Not Pressure Someone into Giving You His Things

איסור חימוד

MITZVAH **38**

איסור חימוד

Do Not Pressure Someone into Giving You His Things

THE MITZVAH

A person is forbidden to pressure his fellow into giving or selling him an item that he covets.

- לֹא תַחְמֹד
- לֹא תִתְאַוֶּה
- הַתְמָדָה
- תַּרְבֶּה
- קִנְאָה
- כֶּרֶם

SECTION I Introduction to the Mitzvah

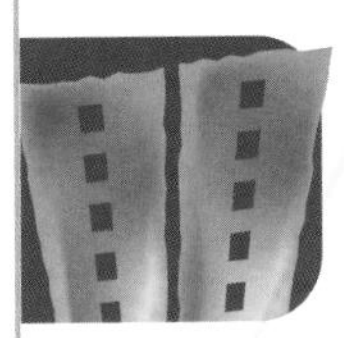

"Sell me that watch! I'll give you $100! No? $200, then! No? I'll give you $500, then! Whatever it takes… I must have that watch!"

A person can want something that belongs to someone else so badly that he will pressure him repeatedly to acquire it. This kind of desire is called חִמּוּד, *coveting*. When the person pressures the owner in an attempt to acquire that item, and finally succeeds, he has violated the prohibition of לֹא תַחְמֹד.

If one person pressures others to acquire their possessions, this shows that he is dissatisfied with what Hashem has given him. He sees others enjoying possessions that he does not have, and becomes filled with jealousy. He plans and schemes how to get the desired object away from its owner, not willing to accept that Hashem does not intend for him to have it.

Hashem wants every person to be happy with what he has in life, and not to look at other people's things and covet them.

How does the מידה of אֵיזֶהוּ עָשִׁיר הַשָּׂמֵחַ בְּחֶלְקוֹ combat לֹא תַחְמֹד?

MITZVAH 25
MITZVAH 26
MITZVAH 27
MITZVAH 28
MITZVAH 29
MITZVAH 30
MITZVAH 31
MITZVAH 32
MITZVAH 33
MITZVAH 34
MITZVAH 35
MITZVAH 36
MITZVAH 37
MITZVAH 38

The Source of the Mitzvah

SECTION II

לֹא תַחְמֹד בֵּית רֵעֶךָ לֹא תַחְמֹד אֵשֶׁת רֵעֶךָ וְעַבְדּוֹ וַאֲמָתוֹ וְשׁוֹרוֹ וַחֲמֹרוֹ וְכֹל אֲשֶׁר לְרֵעֶךָ

שמות כ:יד פרשת יתרו

Do not covet your fellow's house; do not covet your fellow's wife, or his servants, or his maidservants, or his ox, or his donkey, or anything that belongs to your fellow

This פסוק uses the words לֹא תַחְמֹד twice. However, when the עשרת הדברות are repeated in פרשת ואתחנן (דברים 5:18), the Torah uses a different phrase in the second part of the verse. There, the Torah says לֹא תִתְאַוֶּה, *Do not desire* (Mitzvah 416).

According to the Rambam, these two commandments, while closely related, are separate prohibitions. As soon as a person desires another's property and begins planning ways to acquire that property, he has violated the prohibition of לֹא תִתְאַוֶּה, even if he has not set any of his plans into motion. Once he begins to carry out his schemes, he has violated the prohibition of לֹא תַחְמֹד as well (if he is ultimately successful in obtaining the property — see Law 4).

~ *Rambam,* הלכות גזילה ואבידה 1:9-10

According to other Rishonim, even simply desiring another's property is a violation of the prohibition of לֹא תִתְאַוֶּה.

לֹא תַחְמֹד is the last of the עשרת הדברות, but it is connected to the first, אנכי ה' אלקיך. If a person conquers his חִמּוּד for others' possessions, he demonstrates faith in Hashem. The greater the person's faith in Hashem, the less he will covet what is not his.

~ Rabbeinu Bachya in Kad HaKemach, Chemdah

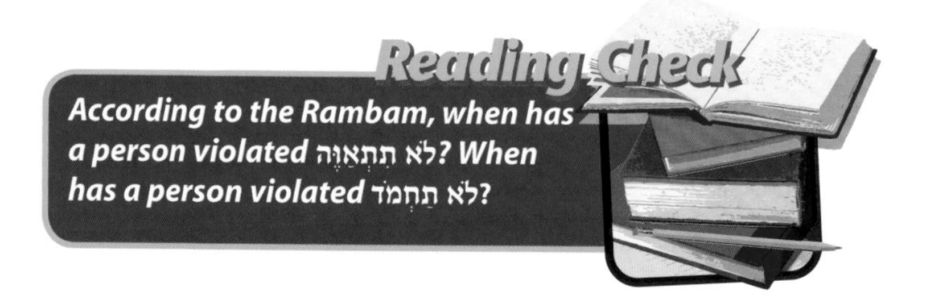

According to the Rambam, when has a person violated לֹא תִתְאַוֶּה? When has a person violated לֹא תַחְמֹד?

A person is forbidden to pressure his fellow into giving or selling him an item that he covets.

SECTION III The Laws of the Mitzvah

1. A person is forbidden to repeatedly ask someone to sell or give him an item that he covets. It is even forbidden to tempt the owner by repeatedly offering him much more money than the item is worth. A person may not do this himself, nor send other people to do it for him. Just desiring another's property is not prohibited by לֹא תַחְמֹד, but may be a violation of לֹא תִתְאַוֶּה (Mitzvah 416).

2. This prohibition applies to properties such as cattle, real estate, slaves, etc., that, when transferred from one person to another, are no longer possessed by the original owner. However, it does not apply to pressuring another person into teaching a skill or a trade, since knowledge is not a transferable object, as the teacher does not lose anything by sharing his knowledge with someone else.

3. The Torah also prohibits a person from coveting his neighbor's wife.

4. A person has violated this prohibition only if his efforts at pressuring the owner are successful, and he actually acquires the item that he covets. A person violates this prohibition even if, in the end, the owner parts with the item willingly.

5. This prohibition applies only when a person tries to acquire the coveted object from its owner. A person is allowed to acquire an identical object from a different source, such as by buying it from a store.

6. This prohibition applies to both men and women, in all places and at all times. As a general rule, all of the Torah's prohibitions (מצוות לא תעשה) apply equally to men and women.

7. A person who violates this prohibition does not incur מַלְקוּת, *lashes*, even if he received proper warning (הַתְרָאָה) and witnesses testified that he did indeed violate it. This is because, as a rule, there is no punishment of מַלְקוּת for violating a לא תעשה whose violation does not involve a physical action (לַאו שֶׁאֵין בּוֹ מַעֲשֶׂה). לא תַחְמֹד is classified as such a prohibition.

טוב טעם
Appreciating the Mitzvah

SECTION IV

A Threat to Society

When a person experiences חִמּוּד and makes no effort to control it, he may become obsessed with satisfying his desires and he will go to any lengths to get what he wants. If he wants to acquire an item that belongs to someone else, he may pressure the owner to sell him the object. If the owner does not sell it to him, he may take it by force. If the owner resists, he might even kill him. Thus חִמּוּד can even lead to murder.

~ *Rambam,* הלכות גזילה ואבידה 10:11

A Life of Frustration

The greatest victim of a person's חִמּוּד is himself. A person who allows חִמּוּד into his heart destroys his own life. Even if he manages to obtain the object of his desire, that will not be the end. There will always be something else to take its place in his heart; as Chazal tell us (קהלת רבה 1:13): No person dies with even half of what he desires in his hands. As time goes on, he desires bigger, better and more expensive things, and he will never be satisfied. He may even endanger his health and his very life to satisfy his urges.

Instead of enjoying the life Hashem has given him, a person in the clutches of חִמּוּד is constantly looking enviously at what other people have, and never finds true happiness. His life becomes a mad rush to attain unreachable goals.

~ see *Migdal David, Sefer Mitzvah, Azharah* §266

A Division between Man and Hashem

Even worse, חִמּוּד drives a wedge between a person and Hashem. Trying to satisfy every desire and acquire

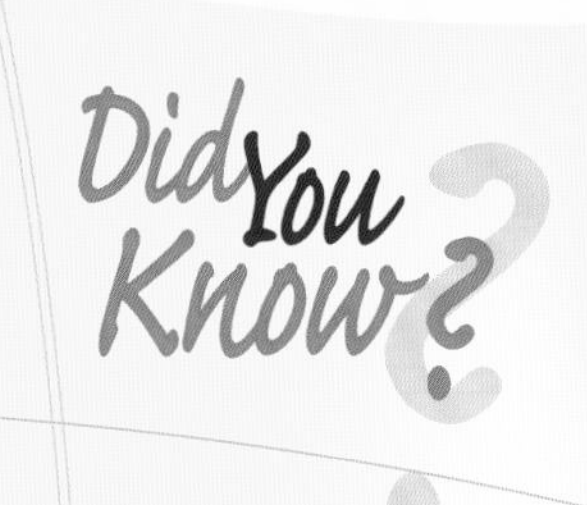

Just as a poor peasant would never dream of trying to marry a princess, we should never covet something that belongs to someone else. For, unless Hashem has decreed that we are to have it, that item is as far from our reach as the princess is from the peasant. One who has true faith in Hashem understands that Hashem gives each person what he is supposed to have.

~ *Ibn Ezra,* שמות 20:14

A person is forbidden to pressure his fellow into giving or selling him an item that he covets.

coveted objects is a time-consuming and money-wasting enterprise, leaving little time or money to devote to Torah and מצוות.

The truth is that a person's money does not really belong to him. Hashem grants a person money to support his family and to live a life of Torah and מצוות. It is not really his money. He is like the teller in a bank who receives the money from the depositor, and must distribute it as the depositor sees fit.

~ *Derech Pikudecha* §38

קנאת סופרים תרבה חכמה

While coveting another's knowledge is permitted by the Torah, coveting someone's Torah knowledge or high level of mitzvah performance is actually praiseworthy. One who covets his friend's Torah knowledge or הַתְמָדָה, *diligence,* will work hard to try to match his friend's accomplishments. This will result in more Torah being studied, and more מצוות being done. For this reason, חִמּוּד of this sort is commendable. This is what Chazal mean when they say: קִנְאַת סוֹפְרִים תַּרְבֶּה חָכְמָה, *Jealousy among students increases wisdom.*

~ *Rabbeinu Bachya,* שמות 20:14

Why is it forbidden for a person to pressure someone to sell him something if he is offering to pay much more than the item is worth?

Living the Mitzvah

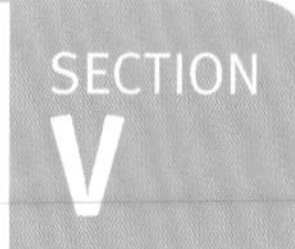

SECTION V

The Story of Achav and Navos

A prime example of חִמּוּד*, which resulted in grave consequences and punishment, can be found in the story of King Achav and Navos. This narrative appears in* ספר מלכים א' *(chs. 21-22).*

The Navi testifies about the wickedness of Achav, מלך ישראל*, "Achav did more to anger Hashem than all the kings of Yisrael who had preceded him," and, "There had never been anyone like Achav, who did what was evil in the eyes of Hashem." Nevertheless, his terrible fate was sealed only because of his criminal behavior toward Navos. This story demonstrates the severity of the prohibition of* לֹא תַחְמֹד *and the severe consequences it brings about. Achav coveted the vineyard of Navos, his neighbor. In Achav's attempts to get it, he became caught up in the sins of theft, false testimony, and even murder. Indeed, Chazal have established Achav as the prime example of a sinful coveter for all generations to come.*

Achav, king of Yisrael, was a great רשע who openly worshipped idols and incited Klal Yisrael to do the same, using false prophets and priests. His wife, Izevel, was even more evil than her husband, constantly urging him to do more עבירות. Indeed, the prophesies of Eliyahu HaNavi constantly urged

A person is forbidden to pressure his fellow into giving or selling him an item that he covets.

Achav and Bnei Yisrael to turn away from עבודה זרה, and to do תְּשׁוּבָה.

Achav had a palace in Yizre'el, and he lived there in kingly splendor. His palace was beautiful, full of riches and surrounded by vast lawns and magnificent gardens, befitting a royal personage. However, Achav was not satisfied with all he had. He wanted more.

Adjacent to the palace grounds, there was a כֶּרֶם, a *vineyard,* owned by Navos the Yizre'eli. Achav decided he wanted this vineyard for an herb garden. He approached Navos and asked him for his vineyard. He offered Navos a superior vineyard in its stead, or its value in silver. This seemed to Achav like a fair and generous offer. However, Navos refused.

"God forbid that I should let you have my family's estate!" Navos replied. This land was his family's יְרֻשָּׁה in Eretz Yisrael, and he did not wish to trade or sell his inheritance.

Achav returned to his palace extremely upset over Navos' refusal to sell him the vineyard. He was so distraught that he had to lie down and he would not eat. When his wife, Izevel, saw him, she was taken aback by her husband's mood. She asked him what was wrong and Achav told her the whole story.

Izevel thought for a moment and then said to her husband, "Is this how you show yourself to be a king? Arise, eat, and let your heart be glad. I shall present you with the vineyard of Navos the Yizre'eli!"

Izevel then wrote scrolls in her husband's name ordering that Navos be framed for a crime he did not commit. She ordered the elders and the officials of the city to declare a fast, for on fast days the elders of the city would sit in judgment. They were then to summon Navos to sit at the table with them. Then, they were to

seat two corrupt men across from him. These men were to testify that Navos "blessed" (this really means the opposite of blessing) Hashem and the king, an offense punishable by death. When Navos would be executed, all of his property, including the vineyard, would be turned over to the king. Izevel then sealed the scrolls with Achav's signet and sent them to the corrupt elders.

The elders of the city received the scrolls and carried out all that was written in them. With Navos seated at the table, the elders listened to the two witnesses give false testimony that Navos "blessed" Hashem and the king; and they immediately carried out the punishment. Navos was put to death.

As soon as Izevel received word of Navos' death, she told her husband, "Go, take possession of the vineyard which Navos the Yizre'eli refused to sell you, for he is no longer alive — he is dead!" When Achav heard his wife's words, he quickly went to take possession of the vineyard.

At this time, Hashem spoke to Eliyahu HaNavi, instructing him to meet Achav in the vineyard and say to him: So says

A person is forbidden to pressure his fellow into giving or selling him an item that he covets.

Hashem, "Have you killed and also inherited? In the place where the dogs licked the blood of Navos, they will lick your blood as well!"

When Eliyahu appeared before him in the vineyard, Achav turned to Eliyahu and asked, "Have you found me, my enemy?" Eliyahu replied, "Yes! I have found you. And since you have devoted yourself to doing evil in Hashem's eyes, Hashem says: I will bring disaster on you and destroy you. I will cut off every male in Achav's family, and all his possessions, whether public or hidden. I will make your house like the house of Yeravam ben Nevat and the house of Baasha ben Achiyah (which were both destroyed), because you provoked Me and caused Yisrael to sin. The dogs will devour Izevel in the valley of Yizre'el. Those of Achav's house who die in the city will be devoured by dogs, and those who die in the open country will be devoured by the birds of heaven."

Sometime after these events, Achav convinced Yehoshafat, king of Yehudah, to join forces with him and wage war against Aram, to recapture רָמוֹת גִּלְעָד. During the war, Achav was mortally wounded. He bled to death, and his blood seeped into the bottom of the chariot. The blood was washed away into the brook of Shomron, and the prophesy was fulfilled when the dogs came to lick the blood of Achav.

Achav's ways were indeed evil and he deserved punishment well before this episode; but his horrible fate was sealed because he coveted and took the vineyard of Navos.

Think & Share

What עבירות can result from coveting another's possessions?

Expand Your Knowledge

SECTION VI

Question: Are there situations in which pressuring someone to part with his property is not a violation of לֹא תַחְמֹד?

The Poskim discuss several situations where it is possible that the prohibition of לֹא תַחְמֹד *does not apply. Some examples are:*

1. *Pressuring someone to sell or give a non-specific item* — לֹא תַחְמֹד only applies to coveting a specific item. Therefore, according to some Poskim, if a child pressures his parents into giving him a birthday gift, but did not ask for a particular item, he did not violate לֹא תַחְמֹד.

2. *Pressuring someone to sell or give an easily obtainable object* — Reuven is very thirsty and can easily go downstairs to the soda machine to buy a soda. However, Shimon just came back from there with an ice-cold soda. Reuven is too lazy to get one himself, and pressures Shimon into selling him his soda. According to some Poskim, Reuven did not violate לֹא תַחְמֹד, because it was not his desire for the soda that made him pressure Shimon into selling it to him, but rather his laziness.

3. *Pressuring someone to sell an object used for a mitzvah* — If someone bought a particularly beautiful אתרוג, according to some Poskim, his friend can pressure him into selling it to him, since it is for the performance of a mitzvah. Others, however, disagree and say that with respect to לֹא תַחְמֹד, there is no difference between mitzvah objects and anything else.

Determine Mastery

REVIEWING KEY INFORMATION

1. What is חִמּוּד?
2. What must a person do to violate לֹא תַחְמֹד?
3. Does a person who pressured another to sell him something violate לֹא תַחְמֹד if: a) he is not successful and does not get the object? b) in the end, the person sells it to him willingly?
4. If someone pressures his friend to teach him how to mow the lawn, is he guilty of violating לֹא תַחְמֹד or not? Why?
5. Why doesn't a person who violated לֹא תַחְמֹד receive מַלְקוּת?
6. How can the feeling of חִמּוּד be used positively?
7. Who is the greatest victim of a person's חִמּוּד? Why?

CRITICAL THINKING

1. How does uncontrolled חִמּוּד contradict faith in Hashem?

Glossary

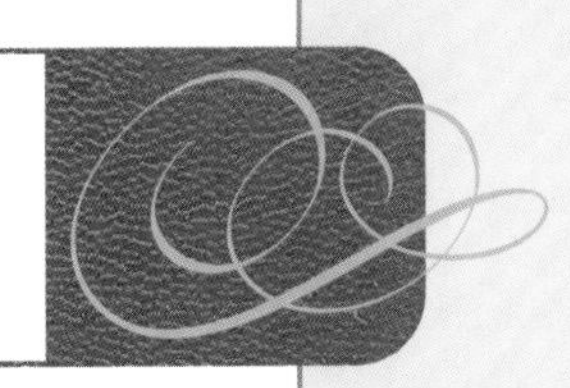

Glossary

A

a·back (adv)
by surprise

a·ban·don (v)
to leave somebody or something behind; to desert

ab·solve (v)
to set free from punishment; to forgive; to pardon; to let off; to excuse

ab·stain (v)
to avoid; to keep from; to give up

ac·ces·si·ble (adj)
easy to reach; handy; available

ac·com·mo·da·tions (n)
housing; quarters; lodgings

ac·com·plish (v)
to bring to a successful finish; to achieve; to attain

ac·cord·ing·ly (adv)
as a result

A·cha·ro·nim
Sages who lived during the fifteenth through twentieth centuries

ac·quire (v)
to get or obtain possession of something

ad·ja·cent (adj)
next to or near; neighboring

a·dul·ter·y (n)
forbidden marriage-type relationship between a man and another man's wife

af·fect (v)
to cause a change in

am·bas·sa·dor (n)
an official representative or messenger; agent

A·mo·ra (n) (pl. A·mo·ra·im)
a Sage who lived during the time the Gemara was written

am·pli·fy (v)
to increase as in volume; to enlarge; to strengthen

an·ec·dote (n)
a brief, interesting story

ar·is·toc·ra·cy (n)
nobility; people of high social class

a·ris·to·crat (n)
a noble; a member of the highest social class of a country

as·pect (n)
point; facet

as·ton·ish (v)
to strike with sudden wonder; to amaze

as·ton·ish·ment (n)
amazement; stunned surprise; wonder

as·trol·o·ger (n)
a person who can tell the future from the position of the stars

a·tro·cious (adj)
extremely wicked; appalling; cruel

at·tain (v)
to reach a goal; to accomplish; to complete

at·test (v)
to give proof; to testify to; to bear witness to

***a·vei·rah* (n)**
sin

awe (n)
fear mixed with respect

B

bar·ren (adj)
empty; desert; desolate

bear·ing (n)
the manner in which one carries or conducts himself; behavior; posture; demeanor

be·fit·ting (adj)
fitting; suitable; proper

be·ra·chah **(n)**
blessing

breth·ren (n)
brothers

budge (v)
to move

bud·get (v)
to set aside; to allocate

bur·den (n)
load; weight

bur·row (v)
to dig

C

cal·i·ber (n)
degree of excellence or importance; worth

cap·tive (n)
prisoner

ca·ra·van (n)
a group traveling together on a long journey through desert or dangerous land

ca·sual·ly (adv)
informally

ce·les·tial (adj)
heavenly

chaff (n)
the seed covering separated from the seed during threshing; husk

char·i·ty (n)
aid to the poor or unfortunate; donations; contributions

Cha·zal (n)
mnemonic for *Chachameinu Zichronom L'Verachah* (our Sages, may they be remembered for blessing). This refers to Sages from the time of the Mishnah and Gemara.

chaz·zan **(n)**
leader of prayers in a synagogue

cher·ish (v)
to love; to hold dear

ches·sed **(n)**
act of kindness

chi·la·zon **(n)**
sea creature from which the blue dye to make תכלת, *blue wool,* comes

cir·cum·stanc·es (n)
the way things happen to be; situation

clas·si·fy (v)
to sort into categories

coax·ing (v)
urging gently; sweet-talking

co·horts (n)
companions; accomplices

col·lat·er·al (n)
property promised as security for a loan

com·mem·o·rate (v)
to remember with a ceremony; to honor

com·mend·able (adj)
deserving of praise; admirable; praiseworthy

com·men·tar·ies (n)
written works that explain other, earlier texts

com·mod·i·ty (n)
a product that is bought and sold; merchandise

com·pas·sion·ate (adj)
sympathetic; kind-hearted

com·pet·i·tor (n)
opponent; rival

complex (adj)
complicated; consisting of many parts

con·cept (n)
thought; notion

con·coct (v)
to prepare by combining various ingredients; to think up; to invent

con·quer (v)
to defeat; to overpower

con·se·quence (n)
result; effect

con·struc·tive (adj)
helping to develop or improve something; positive

con·sume (v)
to burn up; to reduce to nothing; to devour

con·tin·gent (n)
group, especially a unit of soldiers

con·ti·nu·ity (n)
constant flow or progression

con·ver·sion (n)
change from one religion to another

cor·rupt (adj)
dishonest; crooked; unscrupulous

coun·sel (n)
advice; guidance

cov·e·nant (n)
contract; promise; agreement

cov·et (v)
to enviously wish to obtain; to crave

crouch (v)
to stoop or bend low; to squat

cus·tom·ary (adj)
usual; commonly done

D

dank (adj)
damp; wet

de·ceased (adj)
dead

dec·la·ra·tion (n)
statement

de·cline (v)
to refuse

de·duce (v)
to figure out

de·fect (n)
imperfection; blemish; flaw

de·fer·ence (n)
respect

de·grad·ing (adj)
demeaning; belittling

del·e·gate (n)
representative

de·lib·er·ate·ly (adv)
on purpose; with that in mind

delve (v)
to dig

de·mean·ing (adj)
disgraceful

de·pos·i·tor (n)
one who stores money in a bank

de·prive (v)
to take away from

de·rive (v)
to learn from a source

de·scend (v)
to go down

de·scend·ants (n)
offspring from an ancestor

des·e·crate (v)
to treat a sacred place or a sacred object with disrespect

des·ig·nate (v)
to appoint for a special purpose

de·tach (v)
to separate

de·vi·ous (adj)
sneaky; deceptive

de·vour (v)
to swallow up

dil·i·gence (n)
careful and steady work

***di·nar* (n)**
a basic unit of money still used in some countries today

dire (adj)
dreadful; terrible

dis·as·sem·ble (v)
to take apart

dis·ci·ples (n)
students

dis·cred·it (v)
to dishonor; to ruin the reputation of

dis·crep·an·cy (n)
disagreement; contradiction

dis·mount (v)
to get down from

dis·put·ed
contested; debated

dis·suade (v)
to advise against; to talk out of

dis·traught (adj)
very upset; distressed

do·main (n)
territory or property

dram·a·ti·za·tion (n)
a dramatic presentation

ec·stat·ic
overly joyful

e·lab·o·rate
(v) to explain, to go into detail
(n) fancy

em·bark (v)
to begin

em·is·sar·y (n)
representative; agent

***e·mu·nah* (n)**
deep faith and belief

en·a·ble (v)
to allow; to permit

en·dan·ger (v)
to put in danger; to put at risk

en·dure (v)
to last; to live on; to continue

en·sure (v)
to make certain; to guarantee

en·ter·prise (n)
a project

en·thrall (v)
to charm; to fascinate

es·tab·lish (v)
to create; to form; to set up

es·teem (n)
respect; admiration

eu·lo·gy (n)
a formal speech in honor of a dead person

ex·ag·ger·a·tion (n)
enlargement of a fact beyond what is actual or true; overstatement

ex·alt (v)
to glorify

ex·e·cute (v)
to put to death

ex·is·tence (n)
the state of being real; actuality

Ex·o·dus (n)
the departure of the Jewish people from Egypt

ex·or·bi·tant (adj)
beyond the limits of what is fair or reasonable; outrageous

ex·pand (v)
to enlarge

ex·pect·ant·ly (adv)
hopefully; in anticipation

ex·pe·di·tion (n)
a journey or trip taken for a specific purpose

ex·plic·it (adj)
so clear that there is no doubt about the meaning; definite; precise

ex·tend (v)
to stretch out; to make longer

ex·tin·guish (v)
to put out

fab·ri·cate (v)
to lie; to make up

fal·la·cy (n)
a false or mistaken idea; error

fi·ber (n)
thread; strand

firm (adv)
not easily moved or changed

fore·see (v)
to realize what the future holds

for·feit (v)
to give up

for·go (v)
to go without; to give up

for·sake (v)
to leave; to give up; to renounce

fra·grance (n)
a sweet, pleasant smell

ful·fill·ment (n)
accomplishment; completion

fun·da·men·tal (adj)
essential; basic

fu·ror (n)
outburst; excitement

gar·ri·son (n)
troop of soldiers

hag·gle (v)
to dispute or argue over the price

ha·la·chah (n)
Jewish law

halt (v)
stop

haugh·ty (adj)
rudely proud in a way that expresses scorn for others; arrogant; conceited

hav·da·lah **(n)**
separation

hec·tic (adj)
frantic; chaotic

Hel·le·nis·tic (adj)
relating to Greek culture

helms·man (n)
the person at the wheel; driver

hes·i·tate (v)
to pause or stop because of uncertainty or indecision; pause

hes·ped **(n)**
eulogy

high·light (v)
to call attention to; to emphasize

high·way·man (n)
bandit; a person who robs people on a road

husk (n)
thin outer covering of seeds or fruit; shell; hull

I

i·dol·a·try (n)
the worshipping and serving of idols as gods

im·mense (adj)
very great in size or amount

im·merse (v)
to plunge; to bathe; to dunk

im·mo·ral·i·ty (n)
an act that is unethical

im·pact (n)
effect; impression

im·pos·tor (n)
a person who pretends to be someone else in order to deceive; impersonator; phony

im·print (v)
to engrave; to etch; to stamp

im·pu·ri·ty (n)
something that is not pure; contamination

in·ad·ver·tent·ly (adv)
unintentionally; by mistake; without paying attention

in·censed (v)
made very angry

in·ci·dent (n)
happening; occurrence

in·cite (v)
to stir up; to move to action

in·con·se·quen·tial (adj)
not important

in·def·i·nite·ly (adv)
endlessly; continually

in·fa·mous (adj)
having an evil reputation; notorious

in·hab·i·tant (n)
one who lives in a place permanently; citizen; native

in·i·ti·ate (v)
to begin

in·sight (n)
the power to see into or understand a situation; understanding; perception

in·still (v)
to gradually cause to feel or have; to infuse

in·tact (adj)
undamaged; complete

in·ten·si·ty (adj)
extreme strength, force, or feeling

in·tent (n)
purpose; goal

in·ter·min·gle (v)
to mix together; to combine

irk (v)
to annoy

J

ju·di·cial (adj)
relating to courts and judges; legal; official

K

***ke·du·shah* (n)**
holiness

keen (adj)
sharp

ker·nel (n)
a single grain

***kid·dush* (n)**
words of praise recited at the onset of שבת

kid·du·shin
first part of the Jewish marriage process (also known as *erusin*)

kin·dle (v)
to light

knead (v)
to form; to massage; to work; to shape

L

leg·a·cy (n)
inheritance

lest (conj)
for fear that

li·a·ble (adj)
guilty; deserving of

live·li·hood (n)
job; employment; occupation

loop·hole (n)
escape; excuse

loy·al·ty (n)
faithfulness; devotion

***Mab·bul* (n)**
the Flood in the time of Noach

main·tain (v)
to keep in good condition; to keep up; to carry on

***me·for·shim* (n)**
those who explain earlier texts and laws

***me·la·chah* (n)**
literally, labor; especially one of the thirty-nine categories of labor forbidden on שבת

me·mo·ri·al·ize (v)
to commemorate

men·tion (v)
to refer to; to bring up

***Me·rag·lim* (n)**
the twelve spies sent to scout Eretz Yisrael

mer·chan·dise (n)
goods that are bought and sold

***me·so·rah* (n)**
chain of transmission

me·tic·u·lous (adj)
extremely careful; thorough; exact; precise

***Mid·bar* (n)**
desert

***mid·dah* (n)**
character trait

min·i·mum (n)
least

***Mish·kan* (n)**
The Tabernacle

mock·er (n)
someone who makes fun of things

molt·en (adj)
melted by very great heat

mon·arch (n)
ruler

mon·e·tar·y (adj)
having to do with money

mor·tal·ly (adv)
deadly; fatally

***muk·tzeh* (adj)**
literally, set aside; items which may not be moved or handled on שבת

mun·dane (adj)
having to do with everyday life; ordinary; common

ne·go·ti·a·tions (n)
discussions; haggling

ob·li·gate (v)
to require

ob·li·ga·tion (n)
duty

ob·ser·vance (n)
performance

ob·tain (v)
to get; to gain; to acquire; to earn

ob·vi·ous (adj)
easily seen or understood; plain

oc·cur·rence (n)
incident; event; happening

of·fense (n)
crime; sin

P

pal·try (adj)
petty; worthless

par·a·ble (n)
story with a moral or message

par·al·lel (adj)
corresponding to; similar to

per·ma·nent (adj)
lasting or intended to last for a very long time; enduring

per·tain·ing (v)
relating to; concerning; be relevant to

phe·nom·e·non (n)
wonder; marvel

phrase (n)
expression

port (n)
harbor

posh (adj)
elegant; fancy

Pos·kim **(n)**
deciders of halachah

po·ten·tial (n)
possibility; promise

praise (n)
honor; glorify

praise·wor·thy (adj)
worthy of praise; commendable

pre·cede (v)
to come before

pre·serve (v)
to protect; to save

prin·ci·pal (n)
a sum of money that is invested to earn interest

prin·ci·ple (n)
law; standard; truth

pro·claim (v)
to announce

pro·fane (v)
to debase; to desecrate

prof·it·a·ble (adj)
money-making

pro·hi·bit (v)
to forbid

pro·hi·bi·tion (n)
forbidden action; a negative commandment

pro·long (v)
to make longer; to drag out

pro·mi·nent (adj)
eminent; distinguished

pros·per (v)
to do well; to flourish; to thrive

Prov·i·dence (n)
Divine guidance or care

pro·vi·sions (n)
foodstuffs; supplies

pur·suit (n)
chase; hunt

Q

quar·ters (n)
barracks; lodging; rooms

R

re·as·sem·ble (v)
to put back together

re·cede (v)
to move back or away; to retreat; to withdraw

re·cite (v)
to repeat from memory; to narrate; to speak

re·coup (v)
to recover

re·deem (v)
to free from slavery

re·frain (v)
to hold back

ref·uge (n)
haven; retreat; sanctuary

re·gal (adj)
majestic

re·in·force (v)
to strengthen

re·li·a·ble (adj)
worthy of trust; dependable

rep·re·sen·ta·tion (n)
likeness; model

re·sour·ces (n)
means; supplies

re·tire (v)
1. stop working; give up
2. go to sleep

rev·er·ence (n)
deep respect

re·vive (v)
to awaken; to refresh

right·eous (adj)
honorable; just

Ri·sho·nim (n)
early (approximately tenth to fifteenth century) Sages

rite (n)
ceremony

rit·u·al (n)
ceremony

ri·val (n)
adversary; competitor

ruth·less (adj)
brutal; cruel; heartless

S

safe·guard (n)
protection; security

sanc·ti·fy (v)
to set apart as sacred and holy; to consecrate

San·hed·rin (n)
Court of Sages that meets in judgment. It can contain as little as three or as many as seventy-one Sages.

scheme (n)
plot; plan

scoff·er (n)
mocker; someone who makes fun of things

scribe (n)
writer of sacred scrolls

scru·pu·lous (adj)
exact; meticulous; precise

scuf·fle (n)
fight; brawl

sec·u·lar (adj)
worldly; not religious

seep (v)
to ooze; to leak out

sev·er (n)
to end; to terminate

se·vere (adj)
strict; rigid

shear (v)
to cut the hair or wool from animals such as sheep

sheik (n)
an Arab chief

shi·rah **(n)**
song of praise

sieve (n)
strainer

sig·net (n)
a royal seal, usually on a ring

sig·nif·i·cant (adj)
important; meaningful

sin·gu·lar (adj)
individual; single

***so·fer* (n)**
scribe

source (n)
the place from where a law or fact is derived

sow (v)
to plant

splen·dor (n)
brilliance; glory

spur (v)
to urge; to prompt

stip·u·la·tion (n)
condition; qualification

sub·ju·gate (v)
to enslave

sub·merge (v)
to put or go underwater

suc·cumb (v)
to surrender; to give in; to yield

suf·fi·cient (adj)
enough

sus·tain (v)
to maintain; to keep alive; to uphold

sus·te·nance (n)
means of support; nourishment

sym·bol·ic (adj)
representative; a symbol of

sym·pa·thy (n)
pity

T

***ta·chash* (n)**
animal whose colorful hide was used as one of the coverings of the Mishkan

Tan·na (n) (pl. Tan·na·im)
a Sage who lived during the time the Mishnah was written

ter·mi·nal·ly (adv)
fatally

***to·la·dah* (n)**
an act that is forbidden on שבת because it is similar to one of the thirty-nine forbidden מלאכות

trade (n)
business

tram·ple (v)
to flatten; to run over

trans·ac·tion (n)
deal; business

trans·fer·a·ble (adj)
able to be given over or traded to someone else

trans·mit (v)
to send

ty·rant (n)
dictator

***tzad·dik* (n)**
righteous person

***tze·da·kah* (n)**
charity

U

ul·ti·mate·ly (adv)
finally; at last

un·der·mine (v)
to weaken; to sabotage

u·ni·fied (v)
united

un•wa•ver•ing (adj)
steady; consistent; unshakable

val•ian•tly (adv)
bravely; boldly

val•id (adj)
genuine; legitimate

ven•ture (n)
undertaking

ver•bal (adj)
spoken rather than written

vi•cious (adj)
wicked; cruel

vi•o•late (v)
to fail to keep or observe; to break

vi•o•la•tion (n)
breach; transgression

warp (n)
yarn going lengthwise in a loom and crossed by the weft

wa•ver (v)
to shake; to falter

wedge (n)
block; chunk; lump

weft (n)
yarn that crosses the warp threads on a loom

whim (n)
impulse; notion; urge

***yahr•zeit* (n)**
anniversary of a death

צוה כה
ד מצוה כט
מצוה כח
מצוה לג
מצוה לח
מצוה כו